THE LOGICAL MUST

THE LOGICAL MUST

Wittgenstein on Logic

Penelope Maddy

Oxford University Press is a department of the University of Oxford.
It furthers the University's objective of excellence in research, scholarship,
and education by publishing worldwide.

Oxford New York
Auckland Cape Town Dar es Salaam Hong Kong Karachi
Kuala Lumpur Madrid Melbourne Mexico City Nairobi
New Delhi Shanghai Taipei Toronto

With offices in
Argentina Austria Brazil Chile Czech Republic France Greece
Guatemala Hungary Italy Japan Poland Portugal Singapore
South Korea Switzerland Thailand Turkey Ukraine Vietnam

Published in the United States of America by
Oxford University Press
198 Madison Avenue, New York, NY 10016

CIP data is on file at the LOC

9780199391752

1 3 5 7 9 8 6 4 2

Printed in the United States of America
on acid-free paper

For my mother, Suzanne Katherine Lorimer Parsons,
with love and gratitude.

CONTENTS

PREFACE

The aim of this monograph is to examine Wittgenstein's philosophy of logic, early and late, from the perspective a particular brand of naturalism called 'second philosophy'. The Second Philosopher holds a roughly empirical account of logical truth derived from Kant: logic is grounded in the structure of our contingent world; our basic cognitive machinery is tuned by evolutionary pressures to detect that structure where it occurs. The early Wittgenstein of the *Tractatus* also links the logical structure of representation with worldly structure, but insists that the sense of our representations must be given prior to, independently of, any facts about how the contingent world happens to be. When that requirement is removed – as the naturalistically minded will argue that it should be – the *Tractarian* position approaches the Second Philosopher's: logic is grounded in the structure of the world; our representational systems reflect that structuring.

The late Wittgenstein also rejects this priority of sense. The resulting view based on rule-following considerations comes still closer to the Second Philosopher's: both hold that our logical practices are grounded in our interests and motivations, our natural inclinations, and very general features of the world; neither holds logic to be fundamentally different from other descriptions of the world, just more general, responding to features so simple, so ubiquitous, that they tend to go unnoticed. The difference is that the Second Philosopher fills in more of the empirical story. Here she comes up against Wittgenstein's ruling that science is irrelevant, but no principled justification for it can be found in his thought. With this thread removed, Wittgenstein's late view becomes surprisingly naturalistic.

All serious readers of Wittgenstein benefit immeasurably from the writings of those who came before. My own special debts to David Pears and David Stern will be obvious in these pages; what I owe to Barry Stroud, though perhaps less apparent, is no less profound for that. More directly, I've learned a great deal over the years from conversations with Brian Rogers. Discussions in my 2010–2011 seminar on the philosophy of logic first sparked the idea that it might be illuminating to compare Wittgenstein with the Second Philosopher along the lines explored here. Jeremy Heis, David Malament, Patricia Marino, Brian Rogers, Waldemar Rohloff, David Stern, the members of my spring 2013 reading group on the *Philosophical Investigations*, and anonymous referees for Oxford University Press all provided helpful comments on earlier drafts. My heartfelt thanks to all these, and to Peter Ohlin and his reviewers for supporting this unorthodox style of historical engagement. Finally, my gratitude to David Malament, for his friendship and much else, is unbounded above.

P. M.

Irvine, California
January 2014

Introduction

> What you say seems to amount to this, that logic belongs to the natural history of man. And that is not compatible with the hardness of the logical 'must'.
>
> *RFM* VI, §49

The problem of the so-called 'logical must' can be phrased this way: if it's either red or green, and it's not red, then why *must* it be green?[1] Philosophers tend to elaborate by insisting that this isn't the same 'must' as in 'what goes up must come down', that the impossibility of what goes up remaining up is merely physical, not logical. Logical truth,[2] logical necessity are taken to reflect more than what happens to be true in our contingent world: the laws of logic hold in any possible world, perhaps because they actually describe some crystalline realm of pure abstracta. But even without these philosopher's accretions, there's a straightforward question here that confronts any inquirer out to achieve a complete

1. The use of color words here isn't intended to raise the specter of vagueness. If you prefer, feel free to substitute, for example, 'if the switch is either on or off, and it's not on, then it must be off'.
2. Though I speak here and elsewhere of logical truth, no significant contrast with logical validity is intended. In what follows, the question of the truth of 'if it's either red or green, and it's not red, then it must be green', and the question of the validity or reliability of the inference from 'it's either red or green, and it's not red' to 'it must be green', are treated as more or less interchangeable.

understanding the world: why is it that 'if it's red or green, and it's not red, then it's green'?, and what's the added force of the 'must' in 'it *must* be green'?[3]

A few years ago, in a book called *Second Philosophy* [2007], I offered a broadly naturalistic answer to these questions. The 'naturalism' in question is a variant of what's referred to these days as 'methodological naturalism':[4] my Second Philosopher investigates the world beginning from her ordinary perceptual beliefs, gradually developing more sophisticated observational and experimental techniques and correctives, eventually ascending to theory formation and confirmation, all in the sorts of empirical ways usually labeled 'scientific'.[5] In the book, I present the second-philosophical account of logical truth and logical necessity as a descendent of Kant's position, by way of a particular naturalizing move (along with some straightforward Fregean updating). In fact, I think that the same second-philosophical position can be approached from other directions, and in particular, it seems to me that either of Wittgenstein's two characteristic positions in the philosophy of logic – one from the *Tractatus*, the other from the *Philosophical Investigations* and the *Remarks on the Foundations of Mathematics* – provides a viable launching point toward the second-philosophical port. Of course, the naturalizing

3. The question here isn't what makes this truth 'logical', or more generally, what separates logical truths from truths of other kinds. The idea is just to start with uncontroversial examples that everyone would agree count as 'logical', then to ask what makes them true (and what force is added by the thought that they 'must' be true). Also, though relevance logicians don't accept disjunctive syllogism as a general rule, this particular case should satisfy any reasonable requirement of relevance.
4. The contrast is with 'ontological naturalism', which involves a rejection of 'supernatural' entities and causes. See Papineau [2007] for a taxonomy.
5. No demarcation criterion for distinguishing 'science' from 'non-science' is presupposed here – I'm merely describing the Second Philosopher's ways of proceeding in ordinary terms and counting on the reader to get a rough idea of what I'm after. For more on why I take this approach and how it's intended to work, see [2007].

moves required differ in the two cases, as both differ from the one applied to Kant.

Now even if I'm right about this, even if it *is* possible to trace a simple path from Wittgenstein to the Second Philosopher, it's also obvious that not everything doable is worth doing. My hope is that this investigation will prove its worth in two ways, one primary, one secondary. The primary aim is simply historical – to understand Wittgenstein better[6] – but the method is unusual: the idea is to use the Second Philosopher's view of logic, and its roots in Kant, to illuminate Wittgenstein's views on logic, both early and late.[7] If successful, this approach, this atypical perspective, should serve to focus attention in unexpected ways and draw out less familiar features. Along the way, the process of compare and contrast should also reveal new aspects of the Second Philosopher's position – and this is the secondary aim.

The story begins with Kant, and the adjustment that leads to the second-philosophical position.[8] We then turn to the *Tractatus* and finally to the later Wittgenstein.

6. I should admit that I don't believe there to be only one useful way of reading Wittgenstein– which is part of what makes his work so endlessly fascinating – so I give here readings that focus on logic and that seem to me most interesting and productive when viewed side by side with the Second Philosopher's position.

7. There's some difference of opinion on how to partition Wittgenstein's work into periods. All that's needed for present purposes is a rough classification that takes 'early' to include the *Tractatus* and 'late' to include *Philosophical Investigations* and *Remarks on the Foundations of Mathematics*. (Some commentators use the term 'late' for all Wittgenstein's writings from 1929 on; others separate the final writings of 1949–1951 into a 'third Wittgenstein', and recast 'the late Wittgenstein' as 'the second Wittgenstein'. My rough cut leaves room for a 'middle' or 'transitional' period that includes *The Big Typescript*, and involves no stand on the status of *On Certainty*.)

8. For more details, see [2007], §I.4 and Part III. In addition to being much more condensed, the presentation here differs in a few small ways. [201?] summarizes the Second Philosopher's view of logic without the detour through Kant and elaborates a bit further on a few points.

Chapter 1

Kant on Logic

Kant's inquiry in the *Critique of Pure Reason* can be viewed as arising from this question: what must the world be like that we can cognize it as we do? The difficulty of the question increases with his conviction that some of this cognition is a priori:

> It is easy to show that in human cognition there actually are . . . pure *a priori* judgments. If one wants an example from the sciences, one need only look at all the propositions of mathematics; if one would have one from the commonest use of the understanding, the proposition that every alteration must have a cause will do. (B4–5)

Kant notes the obvious problem in his famous letter to Hertz in 1772:

> How my understanding may form concepts of things completely a priori, with which concepts the things must necessarily agree . . . this question . . . is still left in a state of obscurity. (Kant [1772], p. 72)

His solution is the so-called 'Copernican revolution':

> Up to now it has been assumed that all our cognition must conform to the objects; but all attempts to find out something about them *a priori* through concepts that would extend our cognition have, on this presupposition, come to nothing. Hence let us once try whether we do not get farther . . . by assuming that the objects must conform to our cognition, which would agree better with the requested possibility of an a priori cognition of them, which is to establish something about objects before they are given to us. (Bxvi)

Here we see the beginnings of Kant's transcendental idealism.

To sketch the story in crude outline,[1] Kant takes humans to be 'discursive intellects', cognizers who know the world indirectly, via concepts:

> . . . the cognition of every, at least human, understanding is cognition through concepts, not intuitive but discursive. (A68/B93)

The contrasting case of the intuitive intellect is one whose intuition is 'spontaneous',

> . . . as, say, a divine understanding, which would not represent given objects, but through whose representation the objects themselves at same time . . . would be produced. (B145)

Such a God-like intellect actually creates objects by intuiting them, so He cognizes them perfectly without appeal to concepts.

1. For more on the topics of this section, see [2007], §§I.4 and III.2.

At the other extreme, the intuition of the empirical intellect is entirely 'receptive': for such an intellect

> a representation is only a way in which the subject is affected by the object . . . (Kant [1772], p. 71)

Like the intuitive intellect, the empirical intellect also has no need for concepts, this time because the features of its representation are directly stamped upon it by the object.[2] Here the discursive intellect stands apart: it requires an intuitive faculty to connect its cognition to the world; not being divine, its intuitive faculty isn't spontaneous but receptive; not being empirical, its receptive intuition isn't entirely direct, but tempered by its forms of intuition; and it also requires a second faculty, the understanding that spontaneously employs concepts, marks or features 'which can be common to several things' (A320/B377).

It isn't entirely clear why Kant takes a discursive intellect to be the only alternative to the intuitive and the empirical, but however that may be, we now have a fairly detailed characterization of the components of discursive cognition: the 'matter' of experience, which the faculty of sensibility[3] passively receives from the world; the forms of intuition, which automatically organize the raw matter so as to make it accessible to the faculty of understanding; and the concepts supplied spontaneously by the faculty of understanding. The details of the forms of sensibility vary from one type of discursive intellect to the next – ours happen to be spatiotemporal – but the workings of the understanding are the same for all. Furthermore, in another unobvious leap, Kant tells us that any cognition by a discursive knower must take one of twelve

2. Of course, one burden of the *Critique* is to show that this sort of cognition is impossible.
3. A passive, as opposed to spontaneous, intuition is termed 'sensible'.

precise forms – those listed in the Table of Judgments – and that there are twelve corresponding pure concepts available to the discursive knower a priori – those listed in the Table of Categories.

Returning to the original challenge, then, how is it that we humans can know some things about the world a priori, before looking, so to speak? The answer is that the world we experience is partly constituted by our forms of intuition and pure categories, so we can know a priori that it will display the features they determine: for example, the world we experience will be spatiotemporal; it will validate the theorems of geometry and the law of causation, just as Kant thought it should. More generally, the world as experienced by any discursive knower will display the characteristic structures of the forms of judgment and pure categories, though it may not be spatiotemporal.

It's important to recognize that this 'Copernican revolution' wouldn't explain what Kant wanted explained if 'the world we experience' were just a contentious way of saying 'the way the world appears to perceivers with our particular human cognitive systems' – where this is understood as the sort of thing described by empirical psychology. In fact, the findings of cognitive science often report the ways in which our cognitive machinery tends to err, from our susceptibility to optical illusions to our tendency to see physical objects as continuous substance. However basic to our cognition these may be, we obviously don't know them a priori because we don't know them at all – they're false, as careful observation and science have eventually revealed. But Kant's psychology isn't empirical like this; it's transcendental, purportedly telling us the necessary features that the world we experience *must* have. Viewed from this transcendental perspective, the a priori features Kant notes are ideal, due to our contributions, but viewed empirically, from an ordinary or scientific perspective, they are real: the truths of mathematics and the law of causation aren't products of the vagaries of our empirical psychology; they're objective features of the world. Thus transcendental idealism combines with empirical realism.

So where does logic fit into this picture? Though Kant's interests lie elsewhere, in mathematics and in parts of physical science, we've seen the central role played by the logical forms in the Table of Judgments: to take our examples from the relational group, judgments can be categorical ('*A*s are *B*s', subject-predicate form), hypothetical ('if *p*, then *q*'), or disjunctive ('*p* or *q*').[4] To each of the forms of judgment there corresponds a pure category: for example, the category of objects (substance) with properties (accidents) corresponds to categorical judgments; the category of ground and consequent,[5] one substance or situation serving as the ground for another, corresponds to hypothetical judgments.[6] Since the empirical world is partly constituted by the categories, we can know a priori that it consists of objects-with-properties standing in ground-consequent relations; we can know a priori that the world has this much logical structure.[7]

4. For the record, Kant takes disjunctions to be exclusive.
5. In fact, Kant calls this 'cause and effect' (A80/B106), but as a pure category, it can't involve any spatiotemporality. This comes in only later, when the pure categories are schematized to our particular forms of intuition, a process that would presumably go quite differently for a discursive knower with some other forms of intuition. Since our modern-day understanding of causation would seem to involve both spatial and temporal components, I use 'ground-consequent' for the pure category shared by all discursive knowers and reserve 'cause-and-effect' for our own schematized version.
6. Kant's well-known example has 'there is perfect justice' as the ground and 'obstinate evil will be punished' as the consequent (A73/B98). Of course, 'grass is green' doesn't ground '2 + 2 = 4' – 2 + 2 isn't 4 *because* grass is green – despite the truth of the familiar material conditional. See footnote 9 of chapter 2 and the surrounding text.
7. Strictly speaking, pure logic, what Kant calls 'general logic', depends only on the forms of judgment, not the pure categories, which belong to 'transcendental logic'. Still, no world can be cognized with the forms alone – the categories must also be deployed – so a world as experienced by a discursive knower must be structured by both. In the text, I allow myself to speak loosely of the two in combination as 'logical structure'.

To see how this plays out in more detail, notice that our example about red and green is just an ordinary disjunctive syllogism: 'it's red or green' is the major premise; 'it's not red' is the minor premise; and 'it's green' is the conclusion.[8] Each of the three relational forms of judgment noted above provides the major premise for one of the three forms of classical syllogism: categorical, hypothetical and disjunctive. Judging under any of one of these three forms involves adopting a rule, specifically a rule for subordinating an assertion to a condition. As described by Béatrice Longuenesse, these rules are:

> . . . subordination of the predicate to the subject insofar as the latter is the *condition* for the assertion of the predicate [in a categorical judgment], or subordination of the consequent to the antecedent insofar as the latter is the *condition* for the assertion of the former [in a hypothetical judgment], or subordination of the complete division to the divided concept insofar as the latter is the *condition* for the assertion of this division [in a disjunctive judgment]. (Longuenesse [1993], p. 94)

Thus Kant's analysis of what judging consists in reveals that the validity of the corresponding syllogism is actually contained in the act of synthesis required to form the major premise. Longuenesse concludes:

> Syllogism . . . is not a function of thought distinct from that of judging. On the contrary, this function is in some sense 'encased' in every judgment.[9] (Longuenesse [1993], p. 95)

8. Again I'm assuming that even relevance logicians would grant the validity of this instance of disjunctive syllogism (see footnote 3 of the Introduction).
9. She explains this as a second aspect of the priority of judgment for Kant: like concept formation, syllogistic inference, too, comes embedded in acts of judgment (Longuenesse [1993], pp. 92–93).

Syllogistic inference arises from the structure of judgment.

For a particular example, consider the categorical judgment that 'all bodies are divisible':

> . . . being able to think such a judgment is being able to make the inference: 'The concept of the divisible applies to the concept body'; now, the concept of body applies to objects x, y, z; therefore the concept of divisible applies to these same objects'. (Longuenesse [1993], p. 91)

The very act of judging a categorical judgment involves recognizing that if these things fall under the subject concept, then they also fall under the predicate concept. Similarly, to judge a hypothetical involves recognizing that if the antecedent holds, the consequent does, too; in fact, Kant takes the validity of both modus ponens and modus tollens to be present in the hypothetical judgment.[10] The case of disjunctive syllogism is less straightforward, because the inferential content of a disjunctive judgment is actually hypothetical:

> . . . from the truth of one member of the disjunction to the falsehood of the others,[11] or . . . from the falsehood of all members but one to the truth of this one. The former occurs through the *modus ponens* . . . , the latter through the *modus tollens*. (Kant [1800], p. 623)

So our sample logical truth is true because to judge that 'it's either red or green' is in part to recognize that 'it's green' follows from 'it's not red'.

10. See Kant [1800], pp. 622–623.
11. Recall footnote 4.

In this way, because discursive knowers must judge according to the forms of judgment, their acts of judging are necessarily bound by the laws of logic. Those acts of judging can cognize the world because the world experienced by a discursive knower is partly constituted by the structure of discursive thought; it must have this much logical structure and satisfy these logical laws. And since worlds shaped by the logical forms are precisely worlds structured by the pure categories,[12] the laws of logic will be true in any world that consists of objects-with-properties, standing in ground-consequent relations, and so on. Speaking empirically, then, 'if it's either red or green, and it's not red, then it's green' is true because of the way the world is; speaking transcendentally, it *must* be true – a priori, necessarily – because a discursive knower's world *must* have this structure.

If we take one step further and schematize the pure categories, that is, if we bring them in line with our parochial forms of intuition, then object-with-properties becomes spatiotemporal-object-with-properties and ground-consequent becomes cause-and-effect,[13] thus validating also the mathematical and causal truths in Kant's motivating examples. We've seen that these features of the world are empirically real and transcendentally ideal; we now see that logical truths enjoy a similar status, except that the cognitive structures involved in their transcendental ideality include only the logical forms and pure categories[14] common to all discursive intellects, and not, as in the more familiar cases, our specifically human forms of intuition as well. Just as the truths of mathematics can be understood empirically, but the source of

12. See footnote 7.

13. E.g., 'the warmth of the sun' as ground (cause) and 'the melting of the wax' as consequent (effect) (A766/B794). See footnote 5.

14. See footnote 7.

their apriority only transcendentally, the truths of logic can be understood empirically, but the force of the logical must explained only transcendentally. The ordinary scientist comes to know that simple logic is grounded in the way the world objectively is; only the critical philosopher grasps the source of its apriority and necessity in the structure of discursive cognition.

We have here a distinctive account of the nature of logical truth and the force of the logical must. Let's now see how we might go about updating and naturalizing it.

Chapter 2

Naturalizing Kant on Logic

Before undertaking the naturalization process in earnest, we need to face the fact that Kant's syllogistic logic is no longer the most advanced thinking on the subject; we need to update the account of logical form embodied in the Table of Judgments in light of the great innovations introduced by Frege in the *Begriffsschrift* (Frege [1879]).[1] The first of these is the replacement of the Kantian subject-predicate form (for example, '*c* has *P*') with the more flexible multi-place relation or, in Frege's terms, with a function of several arguments ('*R* holds of $c_1, \ldots c_n$'). This allows one among several of these argument to be quantified at a time ('For all *x*, *R* holds of $x, c_2, \ldots, c_n$'), which opens the way in turn for iterated quantifications ('For every *x*, there is a *y*, such that *R* holds of $x, y, c_3, \ldots, c_n$'). For Kant, the quantificational forms are simply 'All *A*s are *B*s' and 'Some *A*s are *B*s' (called 'universal' and 'particular' in the Table of Judgments); the Fregean substitutes would be our familiar and more flexible universal and existential quantifiers. On the logical connectives, such differences as exist between Kant and Frege are less dramatic: negations and conditionals (Frege's term for hypothetical or if-then statements) are common to both,

1. Which isn't to say that Frege thought of his work in this way, that Frege was any kind of Kantian. No stand on this vexed question is intended here.

though we may as well follow Frege in taking negation to operate on entire judgments, not just on the copula. And while we're updating, let's switch to inclusive disjunction and include conjunction as a form of its own.[2]

Adopting these post-Fregean modifications to the Table of Judgments requires corresponding adjustments to the Table of Categories: for example, replacing the logical form subject-predicate with function-and-arguments (or for parallelism, arguments-and-function) goes hand in hand with replacing the category object-with-properties with objects-in-relations. Likewise the form of universal generalization, applied to one place in a judgment, brings with it the category of universality: the property that an object enjoys when it stands in the relations specified by the judgment – that very property holds universally, of all objects. Finally, Frege himself recognizes 'the close affinity' of the conditional form with 'the important relation of ground and consequent' (Frege [1880/1881], p. 37), so there the corresponding category remains the same.[3]

Without following this exercise into its details,[4] it seems fair to conclude that a world partly constituted by our new forms of judgment and pure categories would consist of objects that bear properties and stand in relations to one another; that some of these properties could be universal, holding of all objects; that some

2. Allison ([2004], p. 142) explains why conjunctions – or more precisely the more limited 'copulative judgments' of Kant's day (e.g., 'God has created all things and rules over them' or 'God and one's neighbor should be loved') – aren't included in the Table of Judgments. In the cases of 'hypothetical and disjunctive forms, the component judgments are merely taken problematically within the judgment (neither affirmed nor denied) and only the connection between them constitutes the proposition'. In contrast, 'the elements of a copulative judgment are . . . complete judgmental units . . . that may be affirmed or denied independently of their connection in the judgment. Consequently, their combination does not . . . constitute a distinct moment of thought'.

3. See footnote 6 of chapter 1.

4. For more, see [2007], §III.3.

situations involving these objects would be complements (corresponding to the logical form of negation), conjoinings (corresponding to conjunction) or disjoinings (corresponding to disjunction) of others; and that some interrelations between these situations would be robust ground-consequent dependencies.[5] This much fairly minimal logical structure[6] is enough to validate many classical inferences involving negation, conjunction, disjunction and the quantifiers: introduction and elimination rules, distributive laws, and DeMorgan equivalences, for example.[7] Finally, given that a substantive ground-consequent dependency requires a robust connection between the ground and the consequent, it won't obey the usual equivalences for material conditionals – for example, it may be that either grass isn't green or 2 + 2 = 4, but it doesn't follow that 2 + 2 = 4 *because* grass is green – but at least modus ponens is validated.[8] So the world of our Kant-inspired, post-Fregean knower – call it a Kant-Frege or KF-world – obeys a type of rudimentary

5. Notice that nothing here gives us reason to suppose that worldly indeterminacy or vagueness is ruled out: it seems an open possibility, for example, that an object might not enjoy a given property, but still not fail to enjoy it either. Such gaps would most naturally be regarded as working their way up into complements, conjoinings and disjoinings by the familiar three-valued rules. (That is, the complement of an indeterminate situation is indeterminate; a conjoining obtains if both components obtain, fails if they both fail, and is otherwise indeterminate; a disjoining obtains if one or the other component obtains, fails if both of them fail, and is indeterminate otherwise. These rules are common to strong Kleene and Lukasiewicz three-valued logics; they disagree only on conditionals (here ground-consequent dependencies), which are considered separately below.) Indeterminacy/vagueness seems to me beside the point for the larger themes at issue between the Second Philosopher and Wittgenstein, so I leave it out of the spotlight and make do with a few footnotes (7, 8, 14, 16, and 18). See also [2007], pp. 229–231, 240–244.
6. See footnote 7 of chapter 1.
7. The gaps produce some exceptions: the laws of excluded middle and non-contradiction are indeterminate for indeterminate situations, and reductio ad absurdum is compromised.
8. Modus tollens is not, because of the gaps: if p is a ground for q, and q fails, it only follows that p can't be true; it could be either false or indeterminate.

logic.[9] Speaking empirically, its validities hold because of the logical structure of the world; speaking transcendentally, they hold because of the structure of the (Kant-inspired, post-Fregean) discursive cognition.

With this updated Kantianism in place, let's turn to the problem of naturalization. The need for some such adjustment arises from the two-level structure of the Kant-Frege position outlined here: the Second Philosopher is perfectly at home with empirical inquiry – it's what she does all the time – but transcendental inquiry is another story. Speaking transcendentally, our Kant-Frege theorist tells her, for example, that the existence of individual objects like trees and stones and planets is actually a contribution of her cognitive structuring, not present in the world as it is in itself. This comes as surprising news, but she will, characteristically, reply that she sees no evidence that the physical structure present where that stone is located – a distinct difference in the types of molecules inside as opposed to outside its rough boundary, an electromagnetic field inside that boundary that's strong enough to keep her finger from penetrating the surface when she presses on it, and so on – she sees no evidence that this structure is dependent on her psychology in any way. Of course, the Kant-Fregean replies, speaking empirically, the existence of the stone isn't dependent on anybody's psychology, but I'm speaking transcendentally! The Second Philosopher is open-minded enough not to dismiss out of hand the possibility that there are other methods she hasn't hit upon for finding out what the world is like, so she'll want to

9. Obviously there is some distance between this rudimentary logic and full classical logic. This distance is covered, I suggest, by a series of restrictions and idealizations (including the move from ground-consequent to the material conditional). Since many deviant logics result from rejecting one or another of these adjustments, the debate should focus not on what's true – it's in the nature of restrictions and idealizations to be false – but on what's effective for the purposes at hand (see [2007], §III.7).

know more about this transcendental inquiry, about its scope and methods,[10] but the Kant-Fregean's explanations are unlikely to convince her that his transcendental inquiry is either motivated or viable: for example, no mathematical geometry seems to her to provide a priori knowledge of the world, so she feels no pressure to explain how it does so; and she finds no persuasive account of the methods of 'transcendental' psychology or their reliability. In particular, then, she'll see no strong case for the proposed account of logical truth and the logical must.

This is where the advertised naturalizing move comes in: suppose we simply collapse the two levels into one, viewing both parts of the account empirically, bringing them both within the Second Philosopher's larger inquiry.[11] The result is a position that goes like this: (1) rudimentary logic is true of the world because it's structured as a KF-world, and (2) our basic cognitive machinery detects and represents this KF-structuring (which probably explains why we tend to find the simplest logical connections entirely obvious). As in the empirical level of our Kant-Fregean picture, the structuring in (1) is taken to be fully objective, not something imposed by the machinery in (2), so unless we're inclined to take the structural similarity as an inexplicable coincidence, we should add: (3) human cognitive machinery is as it is *because* we live in a KF-world.

10. This sets her off from naturalists who would reject transcendental philosophy as 'unscientific' from the start; she has no criterion on which to base such a judgment (cf. footnote 5 of the Introduction). For more, see, e.g., [2007], §§I.1 and I.4, or [2011a], §I.

11. I don't pretend that the position generated by so radical an adjustment remains close enough to Kant to qualify as 'neo-Kantian': as we've seen, transcendental psychology can't become empirical without destroying Kant's explanation of why the world of a discursive knower *must* have the relevant features. I also don't intend the naturalized view that emerges to include any other Kantian claims or to rest on any Kantian arguments; it stands as best it can on (descendants of) the three theses to follow. (Thanks to Ethan Galebach for pressing me on this point.)

We have here a candidate for fully second-philosophical position on logic, but is it true? This is a big question – there isn't room for a full accounting here – but let me sketch a rough answer.[12] Taking (1) first, we've derived rudimentary logic as the logic of a KF-world, so the open question is whether or not our world is indeed KF. In fact, as we saw in the Second Philosopher's reaction to Kant's idealism, there is overwhelming evidence of the sort floated there that the familiar physical world of trees and planets, cats and people really does come (roughly) divided into these individual objects. We now add with the same sources of conviction that these objects really do stand in various relations to one another – the cat is in the tree, this person sees the planet – and that some such situations ground others – the apple tree's presence is the result of Johnny's having planted a seed. Indeed, it might seem that tying logic in this way to the structure of a KF-world in fact imposes no constraint, because a logic true in such a world is true in all possible worlds. (This is one of those philosophers' accretions mentioned in the Introduction: logic is necessary.) Another way of putting this is to claim that all possible worlds are KF-worlds, and sure enough, our notion of a possible world is more or less like, say, a model from model theory: a set of individuals with some relations on them. Notice also, that if something like (2) is correct, if KF-structuring is part of our most basic conceptual machinery, it might be difficult for us to imagine a world of a sharply different kind.

Though this is an entirely natural line of thought, I think it's too quick. Of course, for the reasons given, we can expect that it will be hard for us to fully imagine a non-KF 'possible world', but let me try to motivate one such idea nonetheless. Consider (what we might

12. For more, see [2007], §§III.4 and III.5.

call) a Creator World. This notion derives from the intuitionist's Creative Subject, an idealized figure whose mental constructive activities are understood to generate the ontology of intuitionistic mathematics, except that here we imagine the Creator to generate an entire world. In the background, we rely on the machinery of Kripke models for intuitionistic logic as our guide,[13] so that a Creator World will validate a logic different from our rudimentary logic. In particular, it will be a world in which the complement of the complement of a situation needn't be the original situation, in which not-not-p doesn't imply p.[14]

To see this, imagine the Creator acting in a simple, discrete time sequence – t_0, t_1, t_2, . . . – and having powers something like those of Kant's intuitive intellect: by thinking of a thing, he brings it into being. Let's stipulate that he's also quite tenacious: once he thinks of a thing one way, he never changes his mind. Our focus is on the world so generated, the one the Creator's activity brings into being, not on the Creator himself, who remains offstage, behind a curtain, so to speak, like the Wizard of Oz. Such a world couldn't contain changeable human beings like ourselves, so imagine the knower cognizing this world to be a disembodied intellect who experiences the world somehow,[15] but isn't in it.

What is this world like? By thinking a thing *a*, the Creator brings it into being; by thinking of it with property *P*, he brings it about that *Pa*; by thinking of it in relation *R* to object *b*, he

13. See, e.g., Kripke [1965].

14. On the Kleene semantics alluded to in footnote 5, not-p obtains if p fails, fails if p obtains, and is indeterminate if p is indeterminate, so if not-not-p obtains, not-p must fail, and so p must obtain. I focus on this example rather than the more familiar failure of the Law of Excluded Middle, because the truth-value gaps in rudimentary logic also lead to the failure of LEM (see footnotes 7, 16, and 18). But intuitionistic logic is not three-valued logic, or n-valued logic for any n (Gödel [1932]).

15. See footnote 17.

brings it about that *Rab*; and so on for atomic formulas. Now what would it be like, for example, for *a* to fail to have property *P* in this world? It wouldn't be enough for the Creator to have thought of *a* without having thought of it with *P*, for he may wish to leave open the possibility that he will think of it with *P* sometime in the future; if he were to explicitly regard *Pa* as failing now, he could only retain the right to think *Pa* sometime in the future by allowing the possibility of one day changing his mind, which his tenacity clearly prevents him from doing; so he retains that future freedom by leaving *Pa* undetermined, by settling no fact of the matter.[16] For not-*Pa* to obtain now, what he has to do now is decide once and for all that he will never, ever think of *a* as having *P*, perhaps because he can see now that if he did so, he'd have to think something he'd be dead set against thinking.[17] For example, we assume he's dead set against thinking a contradiction, so if he's already thought *Pa*, he can know for sure he'll never think not-*Pa*, so he's sure right now of not-not-*Pa*.

From here, the other Boolean connectives are straightforward: the Creator thinks a disjunction if he thinks one or the other of its disjuncts; he thinks a conjunction if he thinks both

16. This isn't the indeterminacy of vagueness: if it's indeterminate, given Joe's current number of hairs, whether or not he's bald, this is a feature of the property of baldness, not a matter that simply hasn't been settled yet, that might later be filled in (unless, of course, he loses or gains hairs!). At a first approximation, vagueness is better modeled by the three-valued logic of KF-worlds. (Putnam [1983] once proposed intuitionistic logic as a solution to the sorites paradox, but the suggestion meets with difficulties. See Williamson [1996] and the references cited there.)

17. What would the experience of our detached Cartesian observer of this world be like? Hard for us to imagine, surely, but suppose she 'perceives' packets of information sequentially, object-by-object, property-by-property, so to speak, more or less as the Creator creates them. She might first receive the information that an object exists, then that it has some property or bears some relation to an already existing object, later that it lacks another property, etc. In the case at hand, she'd first be aware of *a*'s existence, but still be in the dark about whether or not it has *P*; at some later time, she might learn that it has *P*, that *Pa* obtains, or that it will never have *P* in other words, that not-*Pa* obtains.

conjuncts. Thinking a conditional takes a bit more effort: to think (if *p*, then *q*), he has to consider what would happen if, now or at some future time, he were to think *p*, and conclude that he would then be sure to think *q*. For example, even if he's now uncommitted on *Pa*, he can see even now that if, at some future time, he were to think *Pa*, he would then have to declare himself permanently against not-*Pa*, which is to say, he would then think not-not-*Pa*. So he now thinks (if *Pa*, then not-not-*Pa*). Finally, he now thinks (there is an *x* with *P*) if he thinks of an *a* with *P*. More strenuously, he now thinks (all *x* have *P*) if he considers all the things he thinks of now, and all the things he might think of in the future, and decides that he will think each and every one of them with *P*. For example, if he now thinks not-(there is an *x* with *P*), he can see that if he now or in the future he thought *Pa* for some *a*, he'd also think (there is an *x* with *P*), and since he'd dead set against thinking a contradiction, he knows right now that he'll never do this. So he now thinks not-(there is an *x* with *P*) implies (for all *x*, not-*Px*).

But notice that if he now thinks not-not-*p*, he only commits himself never to think not-*p*, that is, never to commit himself to never think *p*. Whatever mental feat this might involve, it doesn't add up to thinking *p*, so not-not-*p* doesn't imply *p*. And thus it transpires that the logic of a Creator world isn't our rudimentary logic.

But why not? After all, a Creator world has objects-in-relations with ground-consequent dependencies; if this is all it takes to validate rudimentary logic, then a Creator world shouldn't deviate from a KF-world in that respect. This question, the comparison with Creator worlds, drives us deeper into the implicit structure of KF-worlds. Notice first that unlike Creator worlds, KF-worlds have no temporal index: when some aspect of our world is accurately modeled by a KF-structure, what obtains or doesn't obtain depends only on conditions in the present; in contrast (to take just one example), the Creator's negations hinge not only on what he's thought so far, on conditions in the present, but also on what he looks forward to thinking in the future, much of which isn't constrained by his choices up to now. This produces an asymmetry in Creator worlds between *Pa* and its negation, not-*Pa*: for either to obtain now requires a commitment for the future – always to think *Pa* or never to think *Pa*, respectively – but both are commitments involving *P*. No such asymmetry turns up in KF-worlds: there it was simply stipulated that some situations are complements of others; the two situations involved have equal standing, each as the complement of the other; neither enjoys any preferred status. So we see that, in fact, KF-structuring embodies the Boolean idea of negation as a simple toggle, which is why not-not-*Pa* implies *Pa* in our rudimentary logic. This is also why, from a KF point of view, negation behaves strangely in a Creator world: even if the Creator has decided on not-not-*Pa*, he might never get around to thinking *Pa*.[18]

We could consider a different kind of Creator, a Decisive Creator, who prefers, as a general rule, to think of an object *a* as outright lacking any property *P* that he hasn't explicitly thought of *a* as having. If this Decisive Creator were otherwise like our Creator in refusing ever to change his mind, then his world would boil down

18. This type of failure of follow-through on the part of the Creator also explains why he doesn't regard the Law of Excluded Middle as a general rule: though he hasn't thought *p*, as long as he retains the right to think it later, not-*p* doesn't obtain either, and he might want to retain this right forever. As noted in earlier footnotes (5, 7, 8, 14, and 16), KF-worlds also allow for cases in which neither *p* nor not-*p* obtains. Still, as noted in footnote 14, intuitionistic logic isn't a three-valued logic, and we can now see one reason why: intuitionist logic validates not-not-(*p* v not-*p*), but rudimentary logic, with its toggle-like negation, does not. Both agree that not-not-(*p* v not-*p*) is equivalent to not-(not-*p* & not-not-*p*), but for the intuitionist the latter is easily validated – the Creator is dead set against imagining 'not-*p* & not-not-*p*' because he's dead set against imagining a contradiction – while for the rudimentary logician, whenever *p* itself falls in a gap, so do '*p* v not-*p*', 'not-not-(*p* v not-*p*)' and 'not-*p* & not-not-*p*'.

to a series of identical KF-worlds,[19] and rudimentary logic would apply. A more interesting alternative would be a Flexible Creator, who employs the same general rule about negation as the Decisive Creator, counting every property he doesn't explicitly apply to an object as failing to hold of that object, but who allows himself to change his mind, letting an object enjoy a property now but lose it later, and vice versa. Every temporal stage of the Flexible Creator's world would be a KF-world, so again rudimentary logic would apply there, but he'd have to be careful not to mix different stages on pain of contradiction. This would be a world that begins to resemble our own. But neither of these figures is our Creator – he doesn't think decisively or flexibly – and it's the logic of his worlds that we're interested in contrasting with rudimentary logic.

The temporal element and the Creator's own quirks give rise to another contrast in the case of quantifiers. In a KF-world, the quantifiers generalize the simple Boolean disjunction and conjunction, so that (there is an x with P) is equivalent to not-(for all x, not-Px): in particular, if (everything is not-red) fails, then (something is red) obtains. But our Creator thinks differently. He refuses to settle for (there is a red x) unless he's explicitly thought of some a as red. And even if he's decided on not-(for all x, not-Px), he can't be trusted ever to get around to thinking of a particular x with P. For our disembodied cognizers out to investigate this sort of world, again, the rudimentary logic of KF-worlds is not reliable.

But enough of this. All Creator worlds have done, at best, is cast doubt on the necessity of rudimentary logic, on the understanding of 'possible world' that requires KF-structuring; the question we set out to answer – about the viability of (1), particularly the claim that our world is KF – remains untouched by these considerations.

19. Indeed gap-free KF-structures.

Concerning that question, we've seen that there's plentiful common sense and scientific evidence that our familiar physical world does have this structure, but there's also an important challenge from the micro-world, the world of quantum mechanical effects. The famous twin-slit experiment casts doubt on our usual understanding that objects move on spatiotemporally continuous paths,[20] but to revert to Kantian terms for a moment, this would challenge the universality of our human forms of intuition, not the more general notion of object common to all discursive intellects, whatever form their particular sensibility might take – and the reliability of logic depends only on the latter. Restated in second-philosophical terms, this becomes part of our current claim (1), that the reliability of rudimentary logic rests only on the world's KF-structuring and, in particular, not on its spatiotemporal features. Other anomalies, however, do strike at the heart of the pure categories (Kant) or KF-structuring (the Second Philosopher): for example, quantum statistics call the notion of an individual object into question,[21] and the Stern-Gerlach experiments cast doubt on the sense in which particles can properly be said to have properties in the usual (KF) ways.[22]

20. The problem is that it seems impossible to ascribe a continuous trajectory to an electron traveling between a source and a screen separated by a barrier with two slits. See [2007], pp. 236–237, for discussion and references.

21. Suppose we flip two coins identical in composition, shape, weight, etc. Then the probability of an outcome with exactly one head is ½, because two of the four equi-probable possibilities meet that description (that is, first coin heads, second tails, and first coin tails, second heads). But with two subatomic particles of equal mass, charge, spin, etc., the statistics don't seem to distinguish between the state with the particles in one order and the state with the particles in the reverse order. See [2007], p. 237, for discussion and references.

22. This is described briefly in the following paragraph (see also [2007], pp. 238–239). Quantum mechanics also presents difficulties for our usual notions of dependency – some correlations appear not to take any of the forms we're familiar with, not causal, not semantic, not logical – but I won't follow up on this line here (see [2007], pp. 239–240).

If this is right, and if logic does depend on the sort of KF-structuring that's not clearly present in the micro-world, then we should expect breakdowns in rudimentary logic there, and this is just what we do find. For example, in the Stern-Gerlach case, we have good reason to suppose that electrons have spin up or spin down, spin right or spin left, that is, for a given electron *a*, (either *a* is spin up or *a* is spin down) and (either *a* is spin left or *a* is spin right). What the experiments show is that each of the disjuncts of ((*a* is spin up and spin left) or (a is spin up and spin right) or (a is spin down and spin left) or (a is spin down and spin right)) – all four of these disjuncts fail. Here we see the expected failure of rudimentary logic, in particular, of the distributive law.[23]

It's worth noting, in passing, that we might be able to construct from these ingredients an alternative to Creator worlds for mounting our plausibility argument against the necessity of logical truth;

23. 'Failure' might mean that in this case the law fails outright (the premise obtains and the conclusion fails), or that it forms part of a logical system that can't be successfully applied. There may well be important differences between these two (though see [2007], pp. 279–280), but I use the expressions interchangeably here. Also, I don't mean to suggest that we need to devise some other logic to apply in the quantum world. Perhaps we'll eventually get to this point, perhaps not. (Of course new logics for quantum mechanics have been proposed, but so far without conspicuous success. See [2007], pp. 276–279, for some discussion and references.) For now, we reason perfectly well about the quantum world using the mathematical formalism of Hilbert spaces, which display a perfect KF-structure throughout, and are thus suited to rudimentary logic (and even to full classical logic, for that matter, because the restrictions and idealizations alluded to in footnote 9 hold unproblematically for classical mathematical entities). Finally, I also note that some commentators prefer to say – not that ((either *a* is spin up or *a* is spin down) and (either *a* is spin left or *a* is spin right)) obtains, while ((*a* is spin up and spin left) or (a is spin up and spin right) or (a is spin down and spin left) or (a is spin down and spin right)) fails – but rather that, in this situation, none of the purported disjuncts of the conclusion is meaningful. So the distributive law doesn't fail outright in this situation, because the purported conclusion isn't even well-formed. For my purposes, it's enough that the familiar rudimentary inference from the conjunction to the disjunction isn't generally reliable, because sometimes the disjunction either fails or is ill-formed.

we could try, that is, to conceive an entire world whose behavior corresponds closely to the sort of phenomena we actually witness only in the quantum world. For example, suppose the cognizers in this QM-world perceive only in discrete flashes, and then only one property at a time. Suppose they have reason to believe that the 'objects' of their world come in two colors (say, red and green) and two shapes (say, round and square) and when they arrange their counterpart to Stern-Gerlach experiments, they come to see that the distributive law is false.[24]

I won't go into any more detail on Creator worlds or QM-worlds, because we can now also see that there's actually not much point in this exercise. We've noted that these imaginary examples are really just challenges to our intuitive sense that non-KF-worlds aren't possible, to our intuitive understanding of what counts as 'possible'. To support the contingency of logic, our actual world is enough all by itself, because, in fact, rudimentary logic isn't universally applicable, isn't true everywhere, and it takes no subtle theory of modality to conclude that what isn't true isn't necessarily true. KF-structuring is best thought of as a kind of template, one that fits onto some situations and not onto others. Where it does fit, rudimentary logic is reliable. Elsewhere, it is not.

In any case, the moral for (1) is that we can't assume all aspects of our world display the kind of KF-structuring that underlies rudimentary logic. So (1) should be modified to: (1') rudimentary logic is true of the world insofar as it is a KF-world, which in many but not all respects it is. (2) then becomes (2'): our basic cognitive machinery detects and represents (some of) such KF-structuring as there is in the world.

24. In fact, if the cognizers of this QM-world evolved in anything like the way we evolved in our world (see below), presumably they wouldn't feel any inclination to believe the distributive laws in the first place.

An impressive range of evidence in contemporary cognitive science suggests that (2') is true.[25] Current work supports the notion that prelinguistic infants, given ordinary maturation (as opposed to learning), perceive a world of cohesive, solid bodies that travel on continuous paths and preserve their identity through time and when out of sight. The leading theory traces this ability to a mid-level system (a system between the purely sensory and the conceptual) that opens a so-called 'object file' when an object is first noticed, then tracks that individual separately from others even before particular properties are assigned and included in the file. (A canonical illustration of the function of an object file in adults is expressed in the familiar exclamation: 'It's a bird, it's a plane, it's Superman!' The object is individuated and tracked well before any further properties can be successfully attributed to it.) Very young children, again by ordinary maturation, are also capable of classifying objects by their features, individual and relational,[26] and of recognizing both Boolean-style correlations between these properties (that is, of grouping not only by *P* and by *Q*, but also by compounds like (*P* & *Q*) and (*P* v *Q*)) and dependencies between one situation and another. So it seems fair to say that our ability to detect the presence of the world's KF-structures is part of our most fundamental cognitive endowment.

This leaves (3), now modified to (3'): human cognitive machinery is as it is because we live in a largely KF-world and interact almost exclusively with its KF-aspects.[27] For present purposes, it doesn't matter whether these cognitive mechanisms are formed by evolutionary pressures, developed by processes of maturation, or learned

25. See [2007], pp. 245–264, for further discussion and references.
26. Notice that perceiving when an object fails to have a property is implicit in classification by the property in the first place.
27. See [2007], pp. 264–270, for further discussion and references.

in early childhood, but current evidence counts strongly against any dependence on language, or even on experience with manipulating objects in the environment. The stark simplicity of the abilities in question – plausibly essential on the savanna as well as in twenty-first-century civilization – along with their presence in nonhuman animals like birds and primates clearly points toward an evolutionary origin. But let me emphasize that the order of argument here doesn't follow the well-known fallacious line: these cognitive mechanisms have evolved, therefore they must deliver truths. In contrast, the case here begins from evidence that much of the world has KF-structuring and that humans come equipped to detect and represent that structuring very early in life. If evolution enters the story at all, it's well downstream, as an explanation of how our cognitive machinery came to be well-tuned to these objective features of the world (that is, in defense of a particular version of (3')).

Here, at last, we have our second-philosophical account of logic: logic is true of those aspects of the world that enjoy KF-structuring– it can be thought of as a template that fits onto the world when and only when certain conditions are met – so our red or green, non-red object, part of the ordinary KF macro-world, is indeed green. This is a brand of realism – logic reflects objective truths about the world – but without many of the features that typically accompany such realism: logical truth isn't necessary, but contingent on the presence of the requisite structures;[28] logic doesn't describe a world

28. The Second Philosopher is happy to say that the applicability of the logical template, the validity of the logical laws, depends on the presence of KF-structuring. In standard philosophical terminology, this is to say that logic is contingent, but it's worth noting that to say this much, the Second Philosopher needn't (and I think, doesn't) have any developed contrastive notion of metaphysical necessity as many philosophers intend it. (Thanks to Eileen Nutting for pressing me on this point.) In what follows, I use the term 'metaphysical necessity' or just 'necessity' for the philosopher's notion, whatever that might be, and 'logical necessity' and 'physical necessity' for the second-philosophically friendly notions of what's required by the laws of logic and physics, respectively.

of abstracta, but our own familiar physical world. In some sense, our belief in various simple logical connections would appear to be a priori, present before experience; given that our basic cognitive machinery is largely reliable in the familiar macro-world, an externalist epistemologist might take this much logical belief to count as a priori knowledge.[29] But the force of the logical must is compromised: the impression of logic's metaphysical necessity arises from the fundamental role of the relevant cognitive machinery – it's difficult for us to think in non-KF terms, perhaps even impossible (as Kant would have it)[30] – which is why we find KF-structuring built into our very notion of 'possible world' (presumably those who take logic to be metaphysically necessary also take KF-structuring to be necessary). Still, we can make sense of the notion that logical necessity is stronger than physical necessity, because physical necessity depends of features of our world that go beyond its KF-structuring (for example, spaciotemporality, the 'laws' of physics, etc.).[31]

Perhaps it's worth a mention in passing that this naturalization of Kant-Fregeanism produces something closely analogous to a Cartesian position that even generous commentators classify as 'infamous'.[32] Emphasizing God's omnipotence, Descartes

29. See [2007], p. 274. Still, it would take a posteriori investigation of the sort sketched here to reveal that our primitive logical beliefs are true, that our cognitive mechanisms are largely reliable, and thus that these logical beliefs count as a priori knowledge (for the externalist). (Compare: on Kant's view, we empirical inquirers know the truths of mathematics and logic a priori, but we can't appreciate that we do so without engaging in transcendental inquiry.)

30. If so, it seems we may never have a satisfactory understanding of quantum mechanics.

31. Again, this corresponds to the Kantian distinction between dependence on the structure of the discursive intellect and dependence on that plus the spatiotemporal forms of human intuition.

32. See, e.g., Cunning [2006], §3.

held that He could have made the laws of logic other than they are: since 'the power of God cannot have any limits', it follows that

> God cannot have been determined to make it true that contradictories cannot be true together, and therefore that he could have done the opposite. (Descartes [1644], p. 235)[33]

Of course we can't grasp this possibility, because our minds are

> so created as to be able to conceive as possible the things which God has wished to be in fact possible, but not be able to conceive as possible things which God could have made possible, but which he nevertheless wished to make impossible. (Descartes [1644], p. 235)

This view opened Descartes to considerable scorn, as opponents posed riddles like 'could God have made the world independent of Him?', but Margaret Wilson points out that

> [t]here is . . . a lively controversy among some leading philosophers of the present [twentieth] century whether logical necessity might not go the same way as the traditional 'necessity' of Euclidean geometry. (Wilson [1978], p. 126)

She goes on to suggest that

> what is really extraordinary is not Descartes's creation doctrine itself [that is, the doctrine that God created the so-called

33. Cf. Descartes [1630], p. 25: 'he was free to make it not true that all radii of a circle are equal –just as free as he was not to create the world'.

> 'eternal truths'], but the fact that he has not been given more credit for arriving at it. (Wilson [1978], p. 126)[34]

What Wilson has in mind here is Hilary Putnam's claim that, for example, empirical pressures from quantum mechanics might overthrow classical logic, just as empirical pressures from the theory of gravitation once overthrew Euclidean geometry.[35]

Now Putnam's point here is primarily the epistemic claim that logic is empirical, that we could be led to alter our logical beliefs in light of empirical evidence.[36] In contrast, Descartes, like the Second Philosopher, is emphasizing that logic is contingent, that it could have been otherwise.[37] In fact, given that God, having made logic as he has, also made our minds unable to conceive any alternative, it seems unlikely that Descartes could envision Putnam's type of empirical change. Similarly, though the Second Philosopher is less confident than a straight Kant-Fregean that we couldn't come to see the world in terms other than KF-structuring, she does recognize that doing so would mean a difficult and perhaps unattainable shift in our thought processes. Finally, Descartes and the Second Philosopher both take the apparent necessity of logical truth to be an illusion,[38] and their grounds for this are analogous:

34. She proposes a plausible explanation: 'Perhaps the theological basis of his position has stood in the way of a fair historical assessment of the original and important insight it embodies' (op. cit.).
35. See Putnam [1968].
36. If we were so led, we'd come to realize that these logical beliefs weren't true, and hence weren't necessarily true, after all, but this wouldn't automatically preclude our regarding our new logical beliefs as necessary (assuming necessary truths can be known empirically, as many contemporary philosophers do).
37. This position is awkward for Descartes in ways it's not for the Second Philosopher, because Descartes draws such a close connection between conceivability and possibility (see Wilson [1978], p. 126).
38. See Frankfurt [1977]. Of course, commentators disagree on this point (Cunning [2006], §3, gives a summary).

for Descartes, logic appears necessary to us because God made our minds as he did; for the Second Philosopher, logic appears necessary to us because evolution made our minds as it did.[39] So Descartes' position seems more closely analogous to the Second Philosopher's than it is to Putnam's.[40]

If we were to attempt to generate the second-philosophical position from Descartes' position by a single naturalizing move,[41] it would be a familiar one – replace God's benevolent hand with evolutionary pressures from the environment[42] – but this by itself

39. For rhetorical effect, I assume here that evolution is responsible, but as noted above, this is inessential to the second-philosophical position on logic.

40. Conant ([1991], pp. 123–124) draws the parallel between Descartes and Putnam this way: he describes Descartes as thinking it's 'hubris' to suppose that 'an omnipotent God . . . would be . . . bound by the laws of logic', and Putnam as thinking it's hubris to suppose that 'the ongoing activity of scientific inquiry . . . will be forever bound by the laws of classical logic' – in other words, 'science is substituted for God'. The parallel I'm drawing between Descartes and the Second Philosopher is different: for the Second Philosopher, it's hubris to suppose that *the world* is everywhere and always 'bound by the laws of classical logic', whatever may or may not be true of our scientific activity (for now, it's not clear whether or not our theorizing is 'forever bound' by rudimentary logic – it might be). In other words, the world, not our theorizing about the world, is substituted for God. Descartes would clearly agree with the Second Philosopher that the bounds on our thought or theorizing aren't what's at issue in the claim that logic is contingent.

41. The need for naturalization here is different from the case of Kant's transcendentalism. There a new type of inquiry was proposed, and the Second Philosopher was unable to affirm its apparent goals or confirm the reliability of its purported methods. This time around, Descartes is simply adding God as an extra explanatory factor: the world and our minds are as they are because God so exercised his will. The Second Philosopher finds no support for this hypothesis, and considerable support for alternative theories of how the world comes to be as it is and how our minds come to be as they are.

42. My favorite implementation of this strategy would be as applied to Thomas Reid on the sense of smell: 'That all bodies are smelled by means of effluvia which they emit, and which are drawn into the nostrils along with the air, there is no reason to doubt. So that there is manifest appearance of design in placing the organ of smell in the inside of that canal, through which the air is continually passing in inspiration and expiration' (Reid [1764], §II.1, pp. 25–26). How clever of the Almighty, to have placed the organ of smell inside the nose, where the breath is constantly moving in and out!
Notice also that the Cartesian counterpart to the bad evolutionary argument dismissed in the discussion of (3') above is roughly: since a benevolent God gave us these beliefs (faculties), they must be true (reliable). Descartes seems to have fallen for something like this, but arguable Reid did not: 'The Supreme Being intended, that we should have such knowledge of the material objects that surround us, as is necessary in order to our

leaves us with a position much less informative than naturalized Kant-Fregeanism: 'logical truth is contingent on God's will' becomes 'logical truth is contingent on the way the world is', but we're told nothing about which aspects of the world are responsible for the validity of the logical laws or the relevant environmental pressures. Because of his holism, Quine's empiricism about logic has the same defect: no particular features of the world are responsible for the truth of logical laws because no particular features of the world are responsible for the truth of anything; our claims 'face the tribunal of sense experience not individually but only as a corporate body' (Quine [1951], p. 41). Putnam apparently inherits this holistic feature from Quine. In contrast, of course, the Second Philosopher's naturalized Kant-Fregeanism is quite explicit about the KF-structures responsible for both logical truth and logical cognition.

This detour highlights the quite different naturalizing move at work in the central line of derivation we've been following: to generate the second-philosophical position out of Kant-Fregeanism, we simply took a two-level, transcendental/empirical position and collapsed it down to one empirical level.[43] Before the collapse,

---

supplying the wants of nature, and avoiding the dangers to which we are constantly exposed; and he has admirably fitted our powers of perception to this purpose' (Reid [1785], §II.V.10, p. 101). See de Bary [2002], chapter 10, for discussion of Reid on the possibility of God's 'paternalistic deception'.

43. Though perhaps not as widely applicable as the God-to-evolution move, I suspect the two-level-collapse might be effective in other cases as well. Consider, for example, a straightforwardly two-level reading of Carnap [1950]: externally, one chooses, say, the linguistic framework of contemporary science, with its particular logic rather than another, on purely pragmatic grounds; internally, the choice having been made, logic is a priori, true by virtue of the meanings of the words involved. Collapsing the levels produces a view according to which logic is true by virtue of meaning, but the dependence of our meanings on features of human cognition and human practice and their place in the world is acknowledged. This opens the way to the question, why do we have the meanings we do?, which stands to tell us something about the ground of logical truth (see [2012] for a bit more on this line of thought). This theme emerges again below, approached from a different direction.

the logical structures of the world were empirically real and transcendentally ideal. After the collapse, the empirical component remains in place – the logical structures are objective features of the world – but the transcendental psychology – the world is logically structured because it's partly constituted by the forms of discursive cognition – is replaced with an empirical psychology that posits the same cognitive forms, but leaves the world's structure independent. From there, the additions and adjustments required are straightforward: on the worldly side, the vagaries of quantum mechanics need to be incorporated; on the mental side, the correspondence between mind and world needs a new explanation now that the constitutive element has disappeared; overall, empirical evidence for the theory has to be collected and assessed. If I may put it this way, once the collapse is implemented, the rest seems to follow as a matter of course, like a row of dominoes, or falling off a log.

Now let's see how all this looks when we begin from the *Tractatus* instead.

Chapter 3

The *Tractatus*

The *Tractatus* is a work with perhaps as many interpretations as interpreters, leaving room for the occasional agreement or change of mind. David Stern [2003] groups these into rough categories: the logical atomist reading, as a piece of British empiricism (e.g., Russell and Ramsey); the logical positivist reading, as an anti-metaphysical tract (e.g., Carnap and Schlick); the metaphysical reading, as an account of logic and representation (e.g., Anscombe, Stenius, Hacker, Pears); the irrationalist reading, as an ethico-religious work (Janik and Toulmin); and the recently popular therapeutic reading, or 'new Wittgenstein' (e.g., Diamond and Conant). As the parenthetical lists of names suggest, 'the metaphysical reading remains the most widely accepted approach' (Stern [2003], p. 127). Since our focus here is on the nature of logical truth, I'll offer a fairly mainstream metaphysical reading[1,2] as a starting point for the naturalization process.

1. In some regions of the literature, there's an odd tendency to count only realistic readings as 'metaphysical'; e.g., in the opening sections of McGinn [2006], 'anti-metaphysical' seems roughly interchangeable with 'anti-realist'. Morris [2008], pp. 55–58, notes this oddity, and takes the reasonable view that an idealistic reading (which he eventually endorses in his chapter 6, see p. 307) is as metaphysical as a realist reading. White ([2006], pp. 26–28, 98–100) also takes the idealistic option seriously. See chapter 4.
2. Mainstream as it may be, I don't pretend that this reading is without its tensions. Many readers will perhaps agree that the book itself makes some tensions inevitable, but that general fact hardly excuses my particular shortcomings. I hope at least that this take on the *Tractatus* is illuminating for the larger themes of under discussion here. (I've learned most from Pears [1987] and [2006], though I depart from him in ways I won't attempt to catalogue.)

Much as Kant begins from the question, 'what must the world be like that we can cognize it as we do?' the early Wittgenstein can be understood as beginning from the question, 'what must the world be like that we can represent it as we do?' And again as with Kant, the difficulty of the question increases with a conviction about a priority, in Kant's case the conviction that part of our cognition of the world is a priori, revealing necessary features of our world. The counterpart for Wittgenstein is the conviction that the sense of our statements – whether they are capable of truth or falsity, and if so, what it would take for them to be true or false – all this must be given a priori, must be independent of any contingent facts about the world.[3] This simple vision of how language works

3. On the metaphysical side, on the sort of reading I'm attempting here, it seems fully defensible to regard sense as part of the necessary structure of representation: e.g., 'a proposition has a sense that is independent of the facts' (4.061). On the epistemic side, there isn't much to go on in the *Tractatus*, but to separate a priority from necessity here would be to credit Wittgenstein with 'Kripke's . . . discovery of the necessary a posteriori' – characterized by Soames as 'one of the great philosophical achievements of the twentieth century' (Soames [2003], pp. 455–456) – which seems unlikely. Still, the 5.55s present one of those aforementioned tensions. As we'll see below, the sense of a proposition is its agreement and disagreement with the elementary propositions (4.2, 4.21), the 'truth-conditions' of the proposition (4.431); to understand a proposition is to know these truth conditions (4.024); and analysis is what brings out these truth conditions (4.221). Yet (turning to the 5.55s), Wittgenstein also *appears* to think that we can't know a priori 'whether I can get into a position in which I need the sign for a 27-termed relation' (5.5541–5.5542) or more generally that 'I cannot say a priori what elementary propositions there are' (5.5571). I say '*appears* to think' because these passages are actually hedged, but 5.557 tells us outright that 'the *application* of logic decides what elementary propositions there are' and 'what belongs to its application, logic cannot anticipate'. The problem then is this: to reveal the sense of a given proposition, I analyze it down to its truth conditions, to a string of agreements and disagreements with the elementary propositions; but if I can't know what the elementary propositions are a priori, then it seems this process of analysis must not deliver its information a priori. This suggests that the sense of the proposition, which it has of necessity, can't be known a priori. It would be easy to interpret 5.557 to say that while logic can't anticipate what elementary propositions there are, still analysis (for some reason an extra-logical process) is carried on a priori, but the apparent implication of 5.5571 blocks this route. Another possibility is that I can know the sense a priori without knowing its full analysis (5.5562 does suggest that the plain man 'understands propositions in their

was so commonly held at the time as to be nearly invisible, and it remains intuitively appealing even now: what our claims mean, what they say about the world, must be in place first, before we look to the world to determine which are true and which are false.

Commentators locate this idea as part of the doctrine of 'determinacy of sense', which Wittgenstein inherited from Frege:

> There is no doubt that part of the meaning of the postulate, that sense must be determinate, is that there must not be anything contingent in its foundations.[4] (Pears [1981], p. 80)

At the time Wittgenstein himself is perhaps most explicit in the *Notebooks*:

> If a proposition is to make sense then the syntactical employment of each of its parts must be settled in advance ... e.g., what propositions follow from a proposition must be completely settled before that proposition can have a sense! (Wittgenstein [1914–1916], 18.6.15, p. 64e)

As often happens, he's more forthcoming later, when he goes on to reject the idea, as in this passage from the *Big Typescript*:

> There's a misconception . . . language seems to be something that is given a structure and then superimposed onto reality. (Wittgenstein [1933], p. 45e)

---

unanalyzed form'). I won't try to sort this out here; for present purposes, I presuppose, in pre-Kripkean spirit, that a priority and necessity are coextensive, and allow myself to shift back and forth between the two. (Thanks to Thomas Ricketts for helpful conversations on this point.)

4. Of course, another aspect of the determinacy of sense is a rejection of vague boundaries, but as indicated above (see footnote 5 of chapter 2), I leave this idea in the shadows here.

or the corresponding passage from *Philosophical Grammar*:

> Language is not something that is first given a structure and then fitted on to reality. (Wittgenstein [1932–1934], §46, p. 89)

In any case, Wittgenstein's quota of a priority, like Kant's, can be seen as motivating and shaping the resulting philosophy.

The first and most conspicuous appearance of the priority of sense[5] comes right at the start, in the argument for the simple objects that found the system of the *Tractatus*:

> Objects are simple. (2.02) Objects make up the substance of the world. That is why they cannot be composite. (2.021)

Why not? Because

> If the world had no substance, then whether a proposition had a sense would depend on whether another proposition was true. (2.0211) In that case, we could not sketch any picture of the world (true or false) [i.e., we could not represent the world]. (2.0212)

One striking oddity here is that consideration of language inserts itself into the otherwise entirely metaphysical discussion of the 1s and 2s; language only make its official appearance later (at 3.1), as a particular case after the general discussion of picturing in the late 2s and early 3s. I suggest this shows that the priority of sense is functioning behind the scenes even from the outset, and

5. In what follows, I use 'the priority of sense' to encompass both a priority and necessity.

furthermore that the 'argument' of 2.02–2.0212 is only part of a story that reaches its completion in 3.23–3.25.[6]

To see how this works, consider a statement *p* apparently about a complex object *C*, and ask:what is the sense of *p* if *C* doesn't exist? Wittgenstein entertains two options: one is that *p* simply has no sense, describes no way the world must be if it is to be true, unless *C* exists;[7] another is that the claim *C* exists (or better, the claim that some less complex things are arranged in a way that constitutes *C*'s existing) is part of the sense of *p*, as revealed in its analysis. The priority of sense is then deployed in 2.0211 to straightforwardly rule out the first option, because all the senses have to be in place before we look to see whether or not *C* exists (that is, whether or not some other things are arranged so as to constitute *C*'s existing).

The second option remains alive when we reach 3.24:

> a proposition about a complex stands in internal relation to a proposition about a constituent of the complex.

Here we have the parenthetical formulation of the second option: the proposition about *C* 'stands in internal relation' – has as part of its sense – 'a proposition about a constituent' of *C* – that is, any one of the propositions specifying that *C*'s 'constituents' are arranged so as to constitute the existence of *C*. At this point, a simple infinite regress – the sort of thing we see so often in so many areas of

6. This presupposes that the *Tractatus* isn't the simple linear narrative it first appears to be, but many interpreters seem prepared to grant this much.

7. This corresponds to what Frege would call a 'mock thought' as opposed to a 'proper thought' (Frege [1897], pp. 229–230; see also his [1892], p. 157). Though Frege is willing to grant a sense to such sentences, they don't determine a truth value like proper thoughts; he concludes that 'the logician does not have to bother with mock thoughts . . . [but only] thoughts proper, thoughts that are either true or false'. When Wittgenstein speaks of sense, he means the determiner of truth value, so mock thoughts have no sense for him.

philosophy – serves to complete the case: unless this sort of analysis comes to an end eventually, *p*'s sense would never be conclusively settled (before or after looking at the world). Wittgenstein concludes that *p* must ultimately be analyzable into statements that involve only simple names for simple objects, not complexes. Furthermore, if an object at this final level of analysis exists only contingently, the problem of the 2.02s reasserts itself – whether or not *p* has sense depends on the truth of another proposition asserting the existence of that object – but this time, adding the corresponding existence claim at the next level of analysis is no longer an option. In this way, the priority of sense requires that these objects cannot fail to exist. This is the doctrine of simples, the necessary substance of the world.

The first step is now in place: if we're to represent the world as we do, there must be simple objects named by simple names. But this is hardly the full story; as yet we have no account of how linguistic representation is actually achieved. Commentators trace Wittgenstein's answer to this broader question as it emerged from his reactions to Russell's evolving theories of judgment.[8] Russell begins (in [1903]) with the idea that to judge 'Desdemona loves Cassio' is to come into relation with the complex Desdemona-loving-Cassio, but this makes it hard to see how Othello managed, because in fact there was no complex uniting Desdemona and Cassio in love.[9] To fix this, Russell developed the so-called 'multiple relation theory' [1910], according to which Othello comes into relation not with a unified complex, but with Desdemona, Cassio and love. The trouble now is how to distinguish Othello's judging that 'Desdemona loves Cassio' from his judging that 'Cassio loves

8. Here I'm primarily indebted to Pears [1981], [1987], chapter 6, and [2006], pp. 12–15, but see also, e.g., McGinn [2006], pp. 34–41, Morris [2008], chapter 2.

9. The well-worn example comes from Russell [1912], chapter XII.

Desdemona', or worse, from his 'judging' that 'Love Desdemonas Cassio'.

Russell proposed a solution to this problem in [1913]: in addition to the ingredients Desdemona, Cassio and love, Othello must also be acquainted with a 'logical object', the relational form *xRy*.[10] And 'the forms of atomic complexes' aren't alone:

> There are many other logical objects which are involved in the formation of non-atomic complexes. Such words as *or, not, all, some,* plainly involve logical notions; and since we can use such words intelligently, we must be acquainted with the logical objects involved. (Russell [1913], p. 99)

The trouble with this, from Wittgenstein's point of view, is described by David Pears:

> In order to understand the proposition, 'φa', I must be acquainted not only with the property, φ, and the particular, *a*, but also with a logical object, the general form of monadic propositions, ξx. My acquaintance . . . with ξx . . . involve[s] the knowledge *that at least one other proposition of the form is true,* because the only way to achieve acquaintance with a form is to encounter an instance of it. (Pears [2006], pp. 13–14)[11]

10. See Russell [1913], pp. 97–101. A case parallel to 'Desdemona loves Cassio' is treated on p. 99: 'Let us suppose that we are acquainted with Socrates and with Plato and with the relation "precedes" . . . Suppose now that someone tells us that Socrates precedes Plato . . . What we understand is that Socrates and Plato and "precedes" are united into a complex of the form "*xRy*", where Socrates has the *x*-place and Plato has the *y*-place. It is difficult to see how we could possibly understand how Socrates and Plato and "precedes" are to be combined unless we had acquaintance with the form of the complex.'
11. Cf. Pears [1981], p. 79, and [1987], p. 124, which parse the situation somewhat differently.

Wittgenstein was particularly sensitive to this problem because he had considered and rejected something very like Russell's move himself:

> I used to think that the possibility of the truth of the proposition φa was tied with the fact $(\mathrm{E}x,\varphi).\varphi x$. But it is impossible to see why φa should only be possible if there is another proposition[12] of the same form. φa surely does not need any precedent. (For suppose that there existed only the two elementary propositions 'φa' and 'ψa' and that 'φa' were false: Why should this proposition only make sense if 'ψa' is true?) (Wittgenstein [1914–1916], 21.10.14, p. 17e, translation as altered by Pears [2006], p. 14)

Pears concludes that

> this is the vulnerable point that Wittgenstein must have attacked when the two philosophers met in May 1913 . . . (Pears [2006], p. 14)

– which eventually led Russell to abandon the manuscript (it was published only in 1984). Of course, here we see the priority of sense at work again: the sense of one proposition can't depend on the truth of another. For Wittgenstein, the sensicality of a proposition is entirely a function of that proposition itself: 'the proposition represents the situation . . . off its own bat' (Wittgenstein [1914/16], 5.11.14, p. 26e).

Wittgenstein concludes that these problems about judgment 'can only be removed by a correct theory of propositions' (Wittgenstein

12. That Wittgenstein means 'true proposition' is clear from the following parenthesis.

[1914/16], p. 122). Returning to his motivating question – what must the world be like that we can represent it as we do? – we see its very form suggests an even broader inquiry, not just into linguistic sense, but into representation in general, and it's at this level that Wittgenstein makes his fresh start. Meditating on that famous courtroom model of a car accident, in which model cars stood in for the real cars and so on,[13] he hit on his key idea: the essence of all representation is picturing; the parts of the picture stand for parts of the world, and the picture represents them as arranged as the corresponding elements of the picture are arranged; a possible arrangement of the picture elements represents a possible state of the world.

The whole edifice of the picture theory of linguistic representation flows from this one flash of inspiration: 'we picture facts to ourselves' (2.1); 'a logical picture of facts is a thought' (3); 'in a proposition a thought finds an expression that can be perceived by the senses' (3.1). We now see that the fundamental link between simple objects and simple names is forged by shared structure:[14] the possible ways an object can combine with other objects into a fact are mirrored in the possible ways its name can combine with other names into a proposition. This tells us a bit more about those mysterious simples:

> If I know an object I also know all its possible occurrences in states of affairs. (Every one of these possibilities must be part of the nature of the object.) (2.0123)

An object, by its nature, has various possibilities of combination, what Wittgenstein calls its 'logical form'; likewise for its name.

13. See Monk [1990], pp. 117–118.
14. At least in part – there remains the question of 2.0233.

This more sophisticated account of naming scales up to an account of representation itself: a proposition is a possible combination of names, that is, a combination permitted by their various logical forms; the analogous combination of objects is also possible, permitted by the analogous logical forms of the named objects; the proposition and the analogous combination of objects share a more elaborate logical form, built up from the particular ways the names and the objects, respectively, are combined; the proposition represents the analogous combination of objects by virtue of their shared logical form. This sets up a stark contrast between naming and representing: a name correlates with a necessarily existing object; a proposition represents a state of the world that may or may not obtain.

The type of proposition discussed so far is an elementary proposition: 'a concatenation . . . of names' (4.22), which 'asserts the existence of an atomic fact' (4.21).[15] These Wittgenstein took to be logically independent (4.211), just as atomic facts are independent (1.21). Pears ([1981], p. 81) suggests that this view traces to the doctrine of simple objects and simple names, because Wittgenstein thought logical connections between 'concatenations of names' could only arise if some of those names referred to complexes: for example, $f(C)$ and $g(D)$ might conflict if the complexes C and D share a component and make incompatible demands on it. If this is the only way two propositions without compound structure could conflict, then obviously they won't, because the names of the concatenation are simple names for simple objects.[16] In any case, whatever its

15. Here and once again below (see footnote 17), I switch from the Pears and McGuinness translation to Ogden's, preferring his 'atomic fact' to their'state of affairs'.

16. Of course, if items like colors are simples, then elementary propositions can conflict without involving complexes. In the *Tractatus*, Wittgenstein took this to show that colors aren't simple (6.3751), but later the so-called color exclusion problem brought down the entire edifice. See Stern [1995], pp. 98–103.

source, once this last plank is in place, 'the totality of existent atomic facts is the world' (2.04),[17] and 'the world is completely described by giving all elementary propositions, and adding which of them are true and which false' (4.26). A state of the world corresponds to what we now think of as a truth-table row.

The sense of any proposition, then, is its 'agreement and disagreement with the truth possibilities of elementary propositions' (4.4), in other words, a specification of which truth-table rows make it true and which make it false. In this way, one proposition can be the negation of another – the truth table rows that make the one true make the other false and vice versa – and similarly, the conjunction or disjunction of two others, and so on.[18] Still, the logical particles aren't names, they don't pick out simples (4.0312), there are no 'logical objects', as Russell had thought (4.441); rather, the particles indicate how the compound proposition carves the full truth-table into the section that makes it true and the section that makes it false. And, finally, among these compounds 'there are two extreme cases' (4.46), tautologies and contradictions. These 'lack sense' (4.461) because they don't carve the truth-table in two, they say nothing, they 'are not pictures of the reality' (4.462).

So here at last we find our example. If it's either red or green and it's not red, then it must be green because once the antecedents are satisfied, the only remaining truth-table rows make 'it's green' true; or to put it metaphysically instead, because once the facts represented in the antecedent obtain, the logical structure of the world guarantees that the fact represented in the conclusion will also obtain. Reasonable as this may sound, the account goes

17. Ogden again, for the same reason.

18. The quantifiers raise a number of difficult interpretive and doctrinal questions for the *Tractarian* Wittgenstein, but fortunately this level of detail doesn't bear upon the broad themes of interest here.

on to classify our example not as true, but as senseless, as saying nothing about the world.

In the hands of the logical positivists, this idea gave rise to the notion that logic is empty, without content, even conventional, but our metaphysical Wittgenstein draws no such conclusion; though a tautology like ours *says* nothing about the world, it *shows* something deep and important:

> The fact that the propositions of logic are tautologies *shows* the formal – logical – properties of language and the world. (6.12)

What our simple example shows is that language and the world share the basic possibilities embodied in 'it's red' and 'it's green', as well as the compound possibilities in 'it's red or green' and 'it's not red', and finally the dependence indicated by the overarching 'if . . . , then . . . '. What makes the statement a tautology is that shared logical form. The 'must' involved springs from the necessity of the logical structuring: the expressible facts of the world are all contingent, but no matter what those facts happen to be, the world is made up of the same necessarily existing simples with the same possibilities of combination, and these possibilities are enough to guarantee that our example is a tautology. And now Wittgenstein has answered his guiding question: this is how the world must be if we're to represent it as we do.

Chapter 4

Naturalizing the *Tractatus*

One feature that Kant's position and Wittgenstein's share, a feature that makes them attractive candidates for our naturalizing efforts, is that for both, the validity of logical laws arises from the structure of our own physical world, not from goings-on in some distinct realm of abstracta. For Kant, the logical structure of the world is cognized a priori; for Wittgenstein, it's shown a priori in the structure of our language.[1] We saw in Chapter 2 that what makes Kant's position unnaturalistic as it stands is its two-level structure: the Second Philosopher's entire course of inquiry resides at Kant's

1. It's also true that for both, representation hinges on sharing this structure: for Kant, our cognitions can represent the world-as-experienced because the pure categories corresponding to the logical forms of judgment help shape that world; for Wittgenstein, a proposition represents the world because it shares logical form with what it represents. Furthermore, the Second Philosopher's approach to logic might be understood as carrying this theme forward. I don't highlight this way of putting things in what follows, retaining the language of 'detecting' rather than 'sharing' structure from chapter 2, to avoid appearing to assume a stronger resemblance between cognition and world than seems appropriate. I do assume that if a cognitive state counts as 'detecting' a worldly structure, it must somehow encode information about that structure, and this is, in a sense, for the state and the worldly situation it represents to 'share structure'. That sense might be fairly attenuated, though, perhaps comparable to the way a Gödel number 'shares structure' with the formula it represents, which is pretty much just that the latter can be effectively recovered from the former. My worry is that the phrase 'shared structure' suggests something closer to resemblance, which would open up a host of venerable questions. For example, both spatial and color vision successfully encode important information about features of the environment, but if the phenomenal is taken into account, as it must be (see, e.g., Hatfield [2003] or [2009], p. 13), then I think it has to be admitted that spatial experience 'resembles' the features it represents in ways that color experience does not (again, see Hatfield [2003]).

empirical level, leaving the transcendental level both problematic and unmotivated. So one place to begin with the *Tractatus* is to ask whether or not it has two levels in this sense. If so, the same naturalizing move might be applicable: collapse the two levels into one.

Some have proposed such a two-level reading of the *Tractatus*, most notably P. M. S. Hacker, who traces the line of influence from Kant to Schopenhauer to Wittgenstein:

> Thus everything the realist wishes to say can be said; and nothing the transcendental solipsist wishes to say can be spoken of. There will be no practical disagreement between them, nor will they quarrel over the truth-values of propositions of ordinary language. But the analysis of such propositions will manifest the transcendental truths that cannot be said. Wittgenstein's doctrine in the *Tractatus* is best described as Empirical Realism and Transcendental Solipsism. (Hacker [1986], pp. 103–104)

Speaking empirically, everything the Second Philosopher says is entirely in order, just as with Kant. There is, however, the transcendental perspective of the metaphysical subject, who resides not in the world, but at the limit of the world, and for whom solipsism is 'quite correct . . . only it can't be *said*, but it makes itself manifest' (5.62).

Whatever the merits of this interpretation, I think it can't be regarded as a two-level position in the relevant sense. For Kant, there are ordinary claims that receive different truth-values at different levels, as, for example, in the case of the raindrop:

> We would certainly call a rainbow a mere appearance in a sunshower, but would call this rain the thing in itself, and this is correct . . . in a merely [empirical] sense. (A45/B63)

Speaking transcendentally, however:

> . . . not only these drops are mere appearances, but even their round form, indeed even the space through which they fall are nothing in themselves, but only mere modifications or foundations of our sensible intuition. (A46/B63)

What the Second Philosopher says empirically about the objective reality of the raindrops, as opposed to the partly subjective character of the rainbow, is entirely correct for her purposes, but from the point of view of the transcendental philosopher, the raindrops, too, are partly subjective or ideal. We've seen (in Chapter 1) that the same is true of logical truths. In contrast, as Hacker himself notes, the transcendental solipsist doesn't believe[2] that the Second Philosopher's claims are correct *for her purposes*; he thinks they are correct, tout court – it's just that they're incomplete, open to revealing transcendental analysis. He isn't positing an independent inquiry, but an addendum to her inquiry (all of it unsayable, of course).

The 'transcendental' component to the *Tractatus*, then, the component that goes over and above what's available to the empirical realist or the Second Philosopher, stands not in contrast to their ordinary claims, but as explication of them. These purely empirical inquirers don't realize it – and can't realize it, given their methods – but their contingent truths about ordinary physical objects are in fact constituted by configurations of necessarily existing simples, configurations revealed by analysis. What we have here isn't a two-level position, with two equally valid, methodologically independent inquiries, but a one-level view whose extra-scientific component extends and enriches the ordinary science.

2. Or gesture toward or whistle. . . .

The situation might look different if traces of Kantian idealism are thought to linger in the *Tractarian* position.[3] Both Kant and Wittgenstein are out to explain how we come to have something a priori: some knowledge of the world for Kant; grasp of sense for Wittgenstein. Kant solves his problem with an account of cognition that involves a role for our forms and categories in constituting the world-as-experienced; the analogous reading would have Wittgenstein solving his problem with an account of representation that involves a role for the logical form of our language in constituting the world-as-represented. Kant preserves his empirical realism by locating the idealism at his methodologically independent transcendental level; if the *Tractatus* were to follow suit, it would do likewise.

In fact, though, I don't think this idealistic way of reading of the *Tractatus* is correct. What Kant discovers in the course of his inquiry into cognition is that the cognizing of a certain kind of intellect, the discursive intellect, involves the participation of certain forms and categories in the constitution of the world-as-discursively-experienced. In contrast, what Wittgenstein discovers in the course of his inquiry into representation doesn't involve any appeal to us or to any broader class of representers, let alone any role for the peculiarities of that class in the constitution of the world. Rather, what Wittgenstein discovers is the essence of representation itself, the core features that underlie any representation, of any kind at all – by us, by any broader class to which we belong, presumably even by God – namely, that it all boils down to picturing. So we can grasp the senses of our claims a priori because linguistic sense is a particular case of picturing, and pictures can

3. See, e.g., Stenius [1960] for a *Tractarian* idealism strongly analogous to Kant's. For more recent discussions, see Morris [2008], pp. 55–58, and chapter 6, White [2006], pp. 26–28, 98–100.

be understood independently of any contingencies. It isn't that we impose structure when we represent; it's that representation can only take place when certain structures are present. This discovery, combined with the simple fact that we do actually represent the world, tells us something objective – about the world and about our system of language.

On this one-level reading, then, the *Tractatus* presents a challenge more Cartesian than Kantian: the Second Philosopher is told of a new method (the Method of Doubt, the method of philosophical analysis) that promises to reveal the hitherto unappreciated underpinnings of her inquiry (the certainties of First Philosophy, the fully articulated senses of her ordinary claims). If this is right, then a different sort of naturalization move is needed.

The thread I propose to pull this time around is the fundamental assumption cast in the previous chapter as the mainspring of much of the *Tractarian* position, namely, the priority of sense. From a second-philosophical point of view, this is simply untrue. The thought isn't just that it's a contingent matter which combinations of sound or ink stand for which worldly items; Wittgenstein quite reasonably admits to this ('the sign, of course, is arbitrary' (3.322)). The second-philosophical point, rather, is that we learn more about the conditions under which a claim is true or false (Wittgenstein's understanding of 'sense') as we learn more about the subject under discussion (I learn more about the sense of 'that's a rose' as I learn more about flowers); indeed, those truth conditions depend in part on contingent facts about that subject matter (the sense of 'that's a rose' depends in part on botanical facts).[4] Any second-philosophical account of meaning or sense – I

4. Stalnaker makes a similar point in the context of possible world semantics. If the sense of a sentence is 'a partition in the possibilities', then Jackson argues that we must be able to effect such a partition 'independently of how things actually are; independently, that is, of which

won't attempt any such thing here! – would surely begin from our interactions with the world and each other, as studied empirically in a range of disciplines, from specializations like psycholinguistics and sociology, to the optics that underlie perception and the cognitive science of language-learning, to relevant sciences of the worldly features being described (like botany), plus, in all likelihood, various interdisciplinary investigations on the interstices of all these. None of this would appear to leave much room for the priority of sense.[5] Wittgenstein's position might have seemed tenable, perhaps even commonplace, back when language was viewed as a gift of the rational intellect, a creature far removed from the beasts, operating in detachment from the world, but the study of human language has since taken a straightforwardly empirical turn, as the investigation of the representation and communication skills of one remarkable sort of animal, inseparable from the world he inhabits.

So what happens to the *Tractarian* position if this key element is removed? As we've seen (in Chapter 3), the priority of sense plays a central role in Wittgenstein's argument for the necessary existence of simple objects, the fundamental building blocks of the

world is the actual'; otherwise 'we really cannot say how things are at all' (Jackson [1998], p. 53). Stalnaker replies that 'we say how things are (or might be) by distinguishing between possibilities, but . . . questions about the actual nature of the things, events, properties and relations we use to describe counterfactual possibilities may be relevant to questions about the nature of the possibilities we have described, and to the question whether we have succeeded in describing a possibility at all. For this reason, empirical evidence may be relevant to questions about what is possible, and how we have distinguished between possibilities' (Stalnaker [2001], p. 635). As the Second Philosopher might put it: we can't divide the possibilities before inquiry begins, because inquiry is needed to determine what the possibilities are.

5. Perhaps 'senses' associated with some words in the vicinity of KF-structuring could be argued to be present or accessible a priori, but even if this case could be made out, it wouldn't extend far into natural language.

Tractarian system. If the sensicality of a statement about a complex can depend on various contingent truths, then the line of thought beginning in the 2.02s and continuing into 3.2s never gets off the ground: the existence of the complex (or the fact of less complex items being so arranged as to constitute the complex) can function straightforwardly as a contingent guarantor of the sensicality of our statement; it needn't be reassigned as a conjunct of an hypothesized logical analysis of the statement; and that logical analysis needn't be protected in turn from infinite regress. In place of the as-yet unidentified simples, to be revealed at the end-point of the as-yet unexecuted logical analysis, Wittgenstein could rest content with ordinary objects and familiar properties and relations.

Pears draws an illuminating contrast between Kant and the Wittgenstein of the *Tractatus* that helps bring home the force of this shift:

> Wittgenstein's ontological conclusion is recondite. . . . we would not expect to find in ordinary factual discourse either the philosophical proposition in which the ontological thesis is expressed or any mention of things of the type which it mentions [i.e., simples]. . . . the framework of factual discourse . . . is remote and unfamiliar to us.
>
> There is here a sharp contrast with the way in which Kant sets up the framework of his system of factual knowledge. The philosophical propositions which he uses for this purpose are, or at least most of them are, not at all recondite, and in the course of an ordinary factual inquiry there might well be mention of the kind of thing which they mention. For example, the proposition 'every event has a cause' was not first formulated by philosophers, and the application of the concept of cause to

> particular cases is something very familiar. So Kant's framework stands out on the surface. (Pears [1969], pp. 46–47)

As we've seen (in Chapter 1), the ontology of Kant's philosophy, viewed empirically, consists of the familiar objects and properties of science and common sense, while the *Tractarian* ontology, and the analysis that purportedly leads us to it, is so deeply hidden that Wittgenstein himself was unable to provide a single example.

So, removing this particular thread from early Wittgensteinian thought removes the need for mystery, restores us to the ontology of everyday life and scientific investigation. This is undeniably a sea change, but faced with the task of assessing what's left of the *Tractarian* position, we find its central inspiration is left unaffected: the idea of picturing doesn't depend on any fine points of a hidden ontology; its source, after all, was a model with toy cars as stand-ins for the real cars in an auto accident. In a case like this – what Wittgenstein calls a spatial picture (2.171) – it's easy to see how a possible arrangement of picture elements corresponds to a possible arrangement of the objects pictured.[6] As noted in the previous chapter, Wittgenstein carries this over to logical pictures, to linguistic representations, and it reverberates through his entire theory of logic and propositions: the only necessity is logical necessity (6.37),[7] the elementary propositions are logically independent (4.211),[8] so the truth-possibilities for elementary propositions form a full truth-table (4.27),[9] the sense of

6. Most of the time, anyway. As Pears remarks ([2006], p. 10): 'it is only marginally possible for a spatial picture to violate this condition (for example, it is violated by some of Escher's work)'.
7. Any logical picture represents a possible situation, so there can't be a necessary connection not reflected in the logic.
8. Otherwise the conflict of two elementary propositions would be a non-logical necessity.
9. None of the combinations of truth values is ruled out by a non-logical necessity.

a proposition is its agreement and disagreement with those truth-possibilities (4.4), 'a proposition is a truth-function of elementary propositions' (5). From here, it's a short step to the doctrine that tautologies say nothing[10] and show the logical structure of the world.[11] What happens to all this doctrine when we remove the assumption that sense is prior and return to the familiar world?

The key move here is the picture theory's claim that every proposition (logical picture) represents a possible situation, the claim carried over from the case of spatial pictures, the claim whose powerful ramifications are sketched in the previous paragraph. Unless Pears's suggestion from Chapter 3 can be filled in,[12] it's not clear that this claim follows directly from the priority of sense, and if it doesn't, then it won't disappear automatically when that premise is withdrawn. Still, I think it's fair to say that the only thing preserving this central assumption from instant refutation is the hidden ontology, which *does* rest on the priority of sense. To cite the famous example, 'it's red and it's green' looks to be a perfectly meaningful proposition that happens not to represent a real possibility. Wittgenstein acknowledges that 'the simultaneous presence of two colours at the same place in the visual field is impossible' (6.3751), so his only hope is that the as-yet unspecified logical analysis of 'point A is red and point A is green' would reveal why this is a contradiction – why, despite superficial appearances, it's not a proper logical picture. Once we remove the priority of sense, once we're returned to the world of ordinary objects and relations, we're forced to admit the obvious: logically (syntactically)

10. Because they don't divide the truth possibilities.

11. Because their logical form, visible in the syntax, matches the logical form of the world.

12. That is, the suggestion that two elementary propositions could only be logically interconnected if they contained names for complexes (e.g., they might make conflicting demands on some shared component of these complexes).

impeccable sentences can fail to represent possible situations, can fail to have sense.[13] What must the world be like in order for an electron to be blue or the moon to have vertical spin up?

If the assumption that syntactic possibilities mirror real possibilities is allowed to lapse along with the priority of sense, removing with it the many downstream consequences rehearsed above, some *Tractarian* fundamentals still remain: 'the world is the totality of facts' (1.1), 'a fact . . . is the existence of states of affairs' (2), 'the configuration of objects produces states of affairs' (2.0272). Within the non-recondite, ordinary ontology, it seems fair to regard 'states of affairs' as simple configurations of objects-in-relations, and to see these as combining truth-functionally into at least the conjunctive, disjunctive and negative situations that form the basis of KF-structures.[14] Generalities present some difficulties for the *Tractarian*,[15] but it's clear that Wittgenstein intends them to be included (5.52), and once non-logical connections are admitted, presumably non-logical ground-consequent dependencies are unproblematic. So it seems this naturalized *Tractarian* position includes something very like the Second Philosopher's objective KF-structuring, which yields something very like our old principle (1): rudimentary logic is true of the world because of its KF-structure.

Notice, by the way, that without atoms, there's no atomism. When simples were part of the story, when they appeared in the final, complete analysis, there was an ultimate level of KF-structuring. But in the naturalized context, with our ordinary physical ontology, there

13. Pears's remark in footnote 6 – 'it is only marginally possible for a spatial picture to violate this condition (for example, it is violated by some of Escher's work)' – continues, '. . . but it is easy for a string of words to violate it' (Pears [2006], p. 10).

14. Neither Wittgenstein nor the Second Philosopher thinks the logical particles correspond to items in these compound situations.

15. As remarked in footnote 18 of chapter 3.

needn't be any preferred level of analysis: KF-structuring can and does appear at various size scales and in cross-cutting features at a single size scale.[16]

Along with this basic ontology, some rudiments of the picture theory also survive: we represent situations in the world, and successful representations share logical structure with what they represent. Here the Second Philosopher would agree, based on the cognitive science reviewed in Chapter 2: we represent KF-structures and our representations somehow encode that structuring.[17] Structured mental representations of this sort play a central role in much of contemporary cognitive science, with the strongest evidence supporting something intermediate between the view that representations are primitive and structureless, and the view that posits a full language of thought.[18] All that's required for present purposes is a way of encoding objects-in-relations and a few simple ways of generating more complex representations from simpler ones[19] – the sort of thing made eminently plausible by animal studies as well as those on pre-linguistic infants.

16. For an example of the first, consider a Fregean example, 'I am able to think of the Iliad either as one poem, or as 24 books, or as some large Number of verses' (Frege [1884], §22, p. 28). On a shelf of individual volumes, the Iliad and Frege's *Grundlagen* could both be regarded as objects, enjoying certain properties (one red, one green) and relations (three books apart); within the Iliad volume, the objects could be 'books', differently propertied (so many lines each) and related (one before the other); within a given 'book', the verses could be the objects of yet another KF-structure. For the second, a deck of cards forms one KF-structure of objects and their suits, another of objects and their ranks, yet another of objects ordered as the deck happens to be stacked. More dramatically, as Quine has observed, a mass of rabbit flesh forms one KF-structure of rabbits and their properties and interrelations, another of undetached rabbit parts (say feet, legs, torsos, heads and ears) and their properties and relations, and still another of rabbit stages and *their* properties and relations.
17. See footnote 1.
18. For a bit more on the subject of this paragraph, with references, see [2007], §III.8.
19. Following up footnotes 1 (and 17), notice that these modes of generation needn't be compositional – e.g., representations of the conjuncts needn't be parts of the representation of a conjunction – it's enough that there are suitable means for getting back and forth between the component representations and the complex representation generated from them.

The naturalized Kantian (2) – our basic cognitive machinery detects and represents this KF-structuring – goes beyond the bare *Tractarian* view simply by filling in the relevant cognitive science. Finally, the third plank (3) concerns the connection between the objective structure posited in (1) and the representational abilities detailed in (2). Here Wittgenstein is largely silent. The most likely account of this connection, an evolutionary story, might be part of what's rejected in 4.1122 – 'Darwin's theory has no more to do with philosophy than any other hypothesis in natural science' – but let me leave this question aside until later (see the Conclusion). For now, the addition of (3) – human cognitive machinery is as it is because we live in a KF-world – appears as a friendly supplement to the naturalized *Tractarian* picture.

Having reconstructed something close to the naturalized Kant-Fregeanism of Chapter 2, the reasoning behind the shift from (1)–(3) to (1')–(3') remains persuasive. The unreconstructed *Tractarian* takes logical propositions to be necessary, in the sense that they're true on all possible situations, but without simples and their attendant theses, with the reinstated ontology of ordinary objects and relations, we've seen there are good reasons to view such KF-structure as the world enjoys to be contingent, and to doubt that all aspects of the world conform to its familiar contours. And, finally, no reason remains to deny that all this can be expressed in language. Wittgenstein is right that 'it's either red or green, and it's not red, so it must be green' doesn't tell us anything about the 'it' involved, or about the properties 'red' and 'green', and that it's being a tautology does show something about the world. But what it shows is contingent and can also be said: it shows that this aspect of the world ('it' and its properties) has the KF-structuring that validates the logical claim. The entire theory behind this can be said, and we've been saying it here.

So, pulling this one thread from the *Tractarian* fabric, removing the one fundamental assumption that sense is prior, produces a more naturalistic version of the *Tractatus*, and from there, a view of logical truth much like the Second Philosopher's can be seen to emerge. Welcome as this may seem – at least to me! – we now face a new puzzle: the later Wittgenstein of the *Philosophical Investigations* and the *Remarks on the Foundations of Mathematics* also rejects this key assumption, but the view of logical compulsion we find in those works doesn't appear to match the Second Philosopher's. This is the puzzle to which we now turn.

Chapter 5

Rule-Following and Logic

Even the most casual reader of the *Philosophical Investigations* and the *Remarks on the Foundations of Mathematics* will appreciate that the author of those pages did not regard the sense of a statement as something that could be grasped a priori, with finality, as something in place of necessity, independently of the facts, and only subsequently applied to the contingent world.[1] Instead we find him musing that –

> [f]or a *large* class of cases of the employment of the word 'meaning' . . . this word can be explained in this way: the meaning of a word is its use in the language. (*PI* §43)

– and worrying at length that nothing we 'grasp in a stroke' could ever encompass 'the "use" which is extended in time' (e.g., *PI* §138). Without this fundamental *Tractarian* conviction, it's not surprising that the case for simples no longer persuades (*PI* §§39, 46–48), that he bridles at our tendency to insert 'a pure intermediary', a proposition, 'between the propositional *sign* and the facts' (*PI* §94) and to expect 'a final analysis of our linguistic expressions . . . as if there were something hidden in them that had to be brought to

1. The late Wittgenstein also leaves behind the other component of 'the determinateness of sense', namely the rejection of vagueness (e.g., *PI* §98). Cf. footnote 5 of chapter 2.

light' (*PI* §91). The collapsing house of cards finally reaches to the *Tractarian* account of logic:

> Logic . . . presents an order: namely, the a priori order of the world. . . . It is *prior* to all experience. . . . It must rather be of the purest crystal. (*PI* §97)

But this 'crystalline purity of logic', he notes, 'was . . . not something I had *discovered'*, but rather, 'it was a requirement' (*PI* §107), indeed 'an illusion' (*PI* §97).

The 'illusion' here is that there is a '*super*-order' between '*super*-concepts' – like 'proposition', 'sense', 'truth' – whereas these words actually 'have a use . . . as humble . . . as that of the words 'table', 'lamp', 'door'' (*PI* §97). The need for these super-concepts ultimately springs, I've suggested, from the fundamental conviction: if sense is to be grasped a priori, it can't simply be a matter of the mundane use of the expression, which we learn in perfectly ordinary ways; it must concern not the ordinary sentence – 'the perceptible sign of a proposition' (3.11) – but the proposition itself – 'a pure intermediary' (*PI* §94); and so on. To get away from all this, 'our whole inquiry . . . must be turned around', and he adds 'on the pivot of our real need' (*PI* §108). The real need motivating our present inquiry is simple: we want to know why, if it's red or green and it's not red, it must be green. The turn-around Wittgenstein proposes is a philosophy that

> [s]peaks of sentences and words . . . no different[ly] from . . . in ordinary life when we say, for example, 'What is written here is a Chinese sentence', or 'No, that only looks like writing; it's actually just ornamental', and so on. . . . We're talking about the spatial and temporal phenomenon of language, not about some non-spatial, atemporal non-entity. (*PI*, after §108)

The Second Philosopher heartily supports this approach, so the question is what view of logical truth Wittgenstein arrives at in this way.

His late treatment of logic is closely related to the famous rule-following considerations, so we need to start there. The central example of the wayward student is well known:

> Judged by the usual criteria, the pupil has mastered the series of natural numbers. Next we teach him to write down other series of cardinal numbers and get him to the point of writing down, say, series of the form
>
> 0, *n*, 2*n*, 3*n*, etc.
>
> at an order of the form '+*n*' . . . Let's suppose we have done exercises, and tested his understanding up to 1000.
>
> Then we get the pupil to continue one series (say '+2') beyond 1000 – and he writes 1000, 1004, 1008, 1012. (*PI* §185)

We all know that 1002 is the correct application of '+ 2' after 1000, that 1004 is incorrect, but we find ourselves challenged to explain why this is so.

A long string of answers is suggested and each is found wanting: a particular feeling (e.g., *PI* §159) or intuition (e.g., *PI* §§186, 213–214), a mental image or paradigm (e.g., *PI* §139), my intentions as instructor (e.g., *PI* §§186–188), one or another explicit formulation of the rule (e.g., *PI* §§189–190), and so on. This line of thought leads to the well-known paradox of §201:

> This was our paradox: no course of action could be determined by a rule, because every course of action can be brought into

> accord with the rule. The answer was: if every course of action can be brought into accord with the rule, then it can also be brought into conflict with it. And so there would be neither accord nor conflict here. (*PI* §201)

In our search for something that determines the correctness and incorrectness of the student's responses, we've apparently discovered that nothing determines the correctness and incorrectness even of my own, the instructor's own, purported applications of the rule!

In the years following the appearance of Fogelin [1976], Kripke [1982] and Fogelin [1987], much scholarly commentary focused on a general line of interpretation that involved a rule-following paradox and a skeptical solution to this paradox, both on analogy with Hume on causation. Whatever the independent interest of this constellation of philosophical ideas – which has continued to draw considerable attention[2] – commentators soon largely agreed that Wittgenstein himself doesn't intend to espouse the 'paradox' of §201 in his own voice, that he means what he says when he begins the second paragraph of that section with the observation that 'there is a misunderstanding here'.[3] The misunderstanding is to think that a rule always needs an interpretation when in fact 'there is a way of grasping a rule which is *not* an interpretation ... but is exhibited in what we call "following the rule" and "going against it"'.

If we return to the wayward student in this spirit, we realize that in fact we aren't left with nothing to say. We tell him that 1004 is the wrong answer, that it should be 1002; we explain that he must

2. See, e.g., Miller and Wright [2002], Kusch [2006].
3. See, e.g., Stern [1994], §2, [2004], pp. 2–5, §6.2, Pears [1988], pp. 442–443, [2006], pp. 27–28, Baker and Hacker [2009], p. xiii. For Fogelin's more recent take on these matters, see his [2009], especially pp. 15–21.

continue to add 2 even after 1000, just as he did before 1000; we give more examples: 1002–1004, 1016–1018, 2000–2002, 8000–8002, . . . ; and so on. We realize that our conviction that he'd mastered '+ 2' was premature, that more training and testing is needed. Of course it could turn out that this particular student is incapable of understanding – nothing I say can *force* him to cotton on – but if that should happen, I'd take it as a bad sign for his future; it doesn't cross my mind to doubt that 1002 is truly the correct answer and that 1004 is incorrect.

Wittgenstein takes these ordinary reactions to be perfectly proper and adequate, but he recognizes that they won't seem so to a philosopher, that they won't even appear to be of the right order, the right genre, to address the problem in question. This philosophical turn of mind is what interests him most:

> If I am inclined to suppose that a mouse comes into being by spontaneous generation out of grey rags and dust, it's a good idea to examine those rags very closely to see how a mouse could have hidden in them, how it could have got there, and so on. But if I am convinced that a mouse cannot come into being from these things, then this investigation will perhaps be superfluous.
>
> But what it is in philosophy that resists such an examination of details, we have yet to come to understand. (*PI* §52)

The philosopher is aware of the ordinary instruction we'd give to the wayward student, but he's convinced that considerations of this sort cannot answer the question, what makes 1002 correct and 1004 incorrect? Because he's so thoroughly convinced of this, he doesn't bother to examine the ordinary considerations, and instead runs off in pursuit of the various options that Wittgenstein proceeds to debunk.[4]

If we resist this impulse, if we keep our heads and attend to the details of what would actually happen in practice, we notice various simple facts, for example:

> I have been trained to react in a particular way to this sign, and now I do so react. (*PI* §198)

Wittgenstein notes how our ability to follow rules, our practice of rule-following, rests on a number of these obvious and very general facts about us: we humans share a range of interests and motivations; we find the same traits salient, the same applications natural; we react to similar training in similar ways. In addition, the viability of our rule-following practices also depends on various obvious and general facts about the world:[5]

4. Cf. Diamond [1986], p. 47: 'the realistic spirit does not then know so well that you cannot get a mouse from rags that it will not *look at* the rags. . . . philosophers miss the details, the rags, that a philosophical mouse comes out of, because something has led them to think that no mouse *can* come out of *that*.' Though I support this reading (see also Baker and Hacker [2005], pp. 131–132), I admit to some small discomfort. The second sentence of the first paragraph of §52 fits perfectly – if I'm convinced that spontaneous generation is impossible, I won't examine the rags; I simply assume the mouse must have gotten in there somehow without our unnoticing – but the first sentence is puzzling: if I'm open to the possibility of spontaneous generation, wouldn't I examine the rags to see how this process works? Why does Wittgenstein have me examining the rags only to disprove that possibility? Of course, if I'm open-minded on the topic, I'll also be keen to rule out alternative hypotheses about the origin of the mouse, but that certainly wouldn't be my only concern.
5. Some commentators take the late Wittgenstein to be an idealist of one sort or another (see Bloor [1996] for a recent overview and discussion). I see no compelling reason for Wittgenstein to reject such commonplaces as these from Stroud's reply to Lear [1984]: 'We all know that, for the most part, thinking does not make it so, and that, in general, something's being so does not require that it be thought to be so – or that anything else be thought to be so either. Many of the things we think – in astronomy, geology, and biology, for example, were so (or were not) long before there were any people or other beings who could have thought anything. Even most of what has actually been thought to be so has not depended on being thought in order to be so. The eruption of Vesuvius

> The process of putting a lump of cheese on a balance and fixing the price by the turn of the scale would lose its point if it frequently happened that such lumps suddenly grew or shrank with no obvious cause. (*PI* §142)

These ordinary facts about our human nature and about the world in which we find ourselves are the grey rags and dust, and they are enough to ground our practice of continuing series, including the correctness of 1002 and the incorrectness of 1004 in continuing '+ 2' after 1000.

This is one instance of Wittgenstein's therapeutic approach to philosophy. Faced with a philosophical problem, our first thought is to resolve it with a new and improved philosophical account of the subject matter in question, but Wittgenstein counsels us to resist this impulse:

> We may not advance any kind of theory. There must not be anything hypothetical in our considerations. All *explanation* must disappear, and description alone must take its place. . . . The problems are solved, not by coming up with new discoveries, but by assembling what we have long been familiar with. (*PI* §109)

This is what Wittgenstein in fact does for the case of rule-following; he simply describes our familiar practices:

> Philosophy just puts everything before us, and neither explains nor deduces anything. – Since everything lies open to view,

in 79 A.D., for example, was in fact perceived and since then has been thought about by many people, but no one supposes that that eruption occurred only because it was seen or thought about, or that it would not have occurred if no one had ever thought about it, or even that its occurrence required that something or other be thought about by someone' (Stroud [1984], p. 83).

> there is nothing to explain. For whatever may be hidden is of no interest to us. (*PI* §126)

> If someone were to advance *theses* in philosophy, it would never be possible to debate them, because everyone would agree to them. (*PI* §128)

While Wittgenstein's description of our rule-following practices is empirical, its power lies not in the obvious facts it calls to our attention, but in its ability to defuse our philosophical puzzlement, to return us to our senses:

> The real discovery is the one that enables me to break off philosophizing when I want to. – The one that gives philosophy peace. . . . A method is demonstrated by examples. . . . – Problems are solved (difficulties eliminated), not a *single* problem. (*PI* §133)

> There is not a single philosophical method, though there are indeed methods, different therapies, as it were. (*PI*, after §133)

In the rule-following case, the method is to display the ordinary answers to our questions and the general facts that ground them, then to uncover the presupposition that blocks us from being satisfied with those answers.[6]

To get at this troublesome presupposition, notice first that the mathematical character of the central example is inessential; we could just as well be discussing the student's application of the

6. For an example of a different therapeutic method, consider the private language argument: Wittgenstein begins from our assumption that we have a coherent notion of what would constitute a private language, then poses a series of ordinary questions about how such a language might work, until we come to realize that we didn't in fact have a viable notion in the first place. See Stroud [1983], [2000a].

term 'rose' or 'game'. Here, too, we might give examples and explanations, test the student's understanding until we're satisfied that he's got the idea, and still be surprised when he finds it natural to call a palm frond a 'rose' (though it is part of a plant), or an election a 'game' (though it does have winners and losers). The issue, in all these cases, is what determines correct and incorrect uses of the general term. In each case, Wittgenstein points out that we have good reasons for rejecting the student's faulty classifications: a rose is the flower of a member of a particular botanical genus (Rosa), with various characteristics, for instance a crucial reproductive role, not shared by palm fronds; games form a looser collection of items, all bearing a family resemblance, but having winners and losers isn't either necessary or sufficient.[7] These practices of naming and classifying wouldn't work if we humans didn't share various interests and practices, didn't find the same features salient, the same connections natural; they wouldn't work if the world itself were too irregular to support them. But we do and it is, so the ordinary training succeeds.

The trouble with this from the philosopher's point of view is that he doesn't want an answer that happens to work for humans as they actually are, that depends on their contingent abilities and inclinations and circumstances; he wants an answer that must work for anyone, in any situation whatsoever – an answer that would work, in short, no matter how wayward our student or his world might be. Cora Diamond puts the demand this way:

> I do not want, do not think I want, something that would in fact, *does* in fact, *do* to explain to someone how to go on. . . . I take it that a specification of what I really mean picks it out,

7. For the former, think of playing catch (*PI* §66); for the latter, the example of elections will do.

> not as might be for another human being, but in a sense absolutely, from *the* possibilities. . . . a philosophical account of what I really mean . . . is . . . an account addressed to someone on whose uptake, on whose responses, we are not at all depending.
>
> An adequate elucidation of what I meant . . . must pick out something in the realm of things-that-might-possibly-be-meant: not possibly-in-human-practice but in some other sense, not dependent on what goes on in our lives. The fact that someone very different from us might take the explanation by examples differently is read as an indication of what there is, absolutely speaking, in the space of things-that-I-might-possibly-mean, so that an adequate account, adequate to represent what I mean, must make plain that those possibilities are excluded. (Diamond [1986], pp. 68–69)

A similar theme sounds in Warren Goldfarb's discussion:

> We give a rule, some examples of its application, and perhaps some further explanations. Yet, for all that, a person 'could' go on in different ways and take himself to be going on the same. This seems to indicate that what we give is insufficient to tell, or to justify, how to go on; and we demand something more. The demand is not for that which in fact succeeds in showing a person, in particular circumstances, how to go on. It is rather for that which picks out the correct continuation in some unconditioned way, by giving that in which the same really consists. (Goldfarb [1985], p. 105)

The philosopher requires, in other words, an account of the sense of our words that doesn't depend on any contingencies.

What these commentators are describing here should sound familiar. As often happens, what Wittgenstein identifies as the bad presupposition, the presupposition that leads the poor philosopher astray, is a view whose pull he himself feels; in this case, it's none other than a central background assumption of the *Tractatus*: the priority of sense. Once this unnoticed presupposition is removed, the ordinary considerations spring back into view, and we have no trouble explaining our meaning and being understood, no doubt whatsoever about the correctness of 1002 and the incorrectness of 1004.

Let's pause a moment at this point to ask how this approach to rule-following would strike the Second Philosopher. She's obviously no partisan of the priority of sense, so her appreciation of the ordinary answers and what grounds them isn't blocked in that way. Again, I don't pretend to a full second-philosophical account of how meanings are fixed, but the sorts of factors Wittgenstein cites would appear, second-philosophically, to be the right places to begin: our interests and motivations, our natural tendencies, general features of the world. Our evolving practice of naming flowers depends, for example, not only on botanical facts, but on the context of our goals and enthusiasms: for purposes of the weekend gardener, this is properly called a geranium, but for scientific purposes, it's really a pelargonium. If large groups of terrestrial plants didn't share structural and life-cycle features, botanical classification itself would be impossible. And so on. Giving a detailed account of how our words correlate with items in the world is a huge challenge, but the general categories of Wittgenstein's grey rags and dust should strike the Second Philosopher as appropriate points of departure.

But now, returning to Wittgenstein, what about logic? First, as a preliminary, there's the issue of which Wittgensteinian texts are most relevant. Discussion of logic in the *Philosophical Investigations* is confined almost exclusively to the meta-philosophical passages §§89–133. Serious treatment of logical truth and logical inference comes only in the *Remarks on the Foundations of Mathematics,* particularly in Part I, where it's interspersed with considerations of rule-following. This material scholars date to the first draft of the *Investigations* – the so-called 'Early Draft' of 1937–1938 – which consists of an early version of the now-familiar §§1–189 of *PI,* followed by an early version of what's now Part I of the *Remarks.* Years later, in 1944, Wittgenstein made two sweeping changes: he developed the rule-following discussion from the opening of the proto-Part I of *RFM* into the full flowering of §§189–242 of *PI,* and he replaced the material on logic and mathematics with the discussion of private language we now know as §§242ff.[8] So we have perhaps imperfect evidence that Part I of *RFM* should be regarded as more authoritative than the rest of that volume (which was selected not by Wittgenstein, but by his editors); that the material on logic, like the private language argument, is intended to grow out of the rule-following discussion; and that Wittgenstein ultimately took his work on logic to be less finished and less satisfactory than his writings on private language. In light of these considerations, I propose to stick primarily to Part I of *RFM,* and to allow myself some unavoidable leeway in guessing how this rough material might be developed.

Turning then to the content of Part I of the *Remarks,* it looks as if logical inference is being presented simply as a particular case of rule-following: we're trained to take *q* as following from *p* and 'if *p,* then *q*', and we go on to draw this inference; we're trained to infer 'it must be red' from 'it's either red or green' and 'it's not red', and we do so. Wittgenstein encourages this thought with remarks like these:

8. See Baker and Hacker [2009], §I.1.

> 'But doesn't e.g. '*f(a)*' have to follow from '*(x)f(x)*' if '*(x)f(x)*' is meant in the way we mean it?' – And how does *the way* we mean it come out? Doesn't it come out in the constant practice of its use? and perhaps further in certain *gestures* – and similar things. (*RFM* I, §10)

> It is important that in our language – our natural language – 'all' is a fundamental concept and 'all but one' less fundamental; i.e. there is not a *single* word for it, nor yet a characteristic gesture. (*RFM* I, §15)

This sounds like just another example – 'all', alongside '+ 2', 'rose', and 'game' – of how our meanings rest on the consistency of our practices, on our shared reactions to training, on what we find natural. After a rule-following discussion that concludes 'However many rules you give me – I give a rule which justifies *my* employment of your rules' (*RFM* I, §113), Wittgenstein's interlocutor protests:

> 'Then according to you everybody could continue the series as he likes; and so infer *any*how!'

To which comes the reply:

> In that case we shan't call it 'continuing the series' and also presumably not 'inference'. (*RFM* I, §116)[9]

Now it's our use of the term 'inference' that's at issue, but the line of thought is clearly intended to run parallel to 'continuing the series "+2"' in the original rule-following discussion.

9. Cf. *RFM* I, §131: 'The laws of logic are indeed the expression of "thinking habits" but also of the habit of *thinking*. That is to say they can be said to shew: how human beings think, and also *what* human beings call "thinking"'

Though the parallel between '+ 2' and universal instantiation, between familiar rule-following considerations and the treatment of logical inference, is clearly present in the text, I don't think it can be the whole story.[10] What's at issue in the case of '+ 2' is the fixation of our meaning or concept: what is it that makes '1002' right and '1004' wrong, according to our notion of '+ 2'? A parallel concern arises in the logic discussion – what is it that makes '$f(a)$' follow from '$(x)f(x)$', as we understand '$(x)f(x)$'? – and a parallel answer is given: we have this practice of inferring; we find certain moves natural; and (presumably) the world is well-behaved (though this part isn't explicit in the passages just cited). But in the case of logic, another concern arises. It isn't just a matter of how we manage to fix our meanings, our rules for inferring; there's also the recognition that some meanings, some rules, are better than others. So, for example, our 'or' and 'not' underwrite the truth-preserving inference from 'it's red or green' and 'it's not red' to 'it's green', but 'tonk' licenses the truth-squandering move from 'it's red' to 'it's red tonk it's green', and from there to 'it's green'.[11] We can fix the meaning of 'tonk' in the same general ways as we manage to fix the meaning of '+ 2' – in fact, we have – but using 'tonk' in place of 'or' and 'not' would lead us astray. Of course, the wayward student goes astray in the context of our use of '+ 2', but embracing 'tonk' would lead our whole practice astray. How we fix meanings is one question; which meanings to fix is another. Or so it seems.

10. If the parallel with private language is to hold true, we shouldn't expect the treatment of logic to be a straightforward application of rule-following considerations: though Kripke ([1982], chapter 3) understands the private language argument in this way, the more therapeutic approach sketched in footnote 6 seems to me more in line with Wittgenstein's intentions. Perhaps both logic and private language are best seen as potential counter-examples to the ordinary answers and simple grounds identified in the story of following a rule, as in Baker and Hacker, 'Two fruits upon one tree', [2009], chapter 1.

11. The introduction rules for 'tonk' mimic those for 'or' – e.g., p implies (p tonk q) – and its elimination rules mimic those for 'and' – e.g., (p tonk q) implies q. See Prior [1960].

Apparently in response to a concern like this, in the early rule-following passages of *RFM*, Part I, we find the interlocutor lodging line of protest that (as far as I can tell) doesn't appear in the *Investigations*:

> 'But isn't there a truth corresponding to logical inference? Isn't it *true* that this follows from that?' (*RFM* I, §5)
>
> But still, I must only infer what really *follows*! (*RFM* I, §8)

To which the response comes:

> Is this supposed to mean: only what follows, going by the rules of inference; or is it supposed to mean: only what follows, going by *such* rules of inference as somehow agree with some (sort of) reality? (*RFM* I, §8)

Naturally the interlocutor means the latter, not 'really follows by our rules' but 'really follows' period: here we have the stark difference between what makes '1002' correct on our meaning of '+ 2' and what makes our meanings of 'or' and 'not' better than our meaning of 'tonk'. Wittgenstein formulates this fresh concern with admirable forthrightness:

> What would happen if we made a different inference – *how* should we get into conflict with the truth? (*RFM* I, §5)

How would using 'tonk' instead of 'or' and 'not' lead us into falsehood?

Armed with our Wittgensteinian respect for ordinary replies, this is hardly a difficult question to answer: if I make the 'tonk' inference from a true premise – 'it's red' – to a false conclusion – 'it's green' – I've come into conflict with the truth. Of course, the wayward student has also come into conflict with the truth when he answers 1004, because he makes this move in the context of our practice of following '+ 2', where it's incorrect, but the case of 'tonk' is different, because we're following the 'tonk' rule correctly; it's just a bad rule. So, the new question is: what makes this a bad rule?

I think Wittgenstein's answer to this question marshals the same considerations as his answer to the question, 'what makes "1004" wrong?' – which is why the two tend to blend together. '1004' is wrong because '+ 2' is embedded in a practice that requires '1002', but now we're asking a question analogous to 'what makes "+2" a good rule in that practice?'. The practice of elementary arithmetic is as it is for a range of reasons, among them that we have certain interests and goals in which counting and the arithmetical operations are important and that we find '+ 2' more natural than a rule that changes to what we call '+ 4' after 1000. The practice of inferring is also based on our interests and goals: we want to know about the world around us; we enhance that knowledge by having a reliable method of moving from truths to truths. There might be nothing particularly disadvantageous about employing an arithmetical rule that changes from our '+ 2' to our '+ 4' after 1000, but a rule that calls for random choices or coin flips at each point would not serve the purposes of the practice of arithmetic. Likewise, there would be nothing particularly disadvantageous about using an exclusive 'or' in place of our inclusive 'or', but using 'tonk' defeats the purpose of inferring. *Both* correct application of existing rules *and* the choice between possible rules rest on the familiar Wittgensteinian trio of our interests, our nature, and the world's regularities.

Though our examples so far have come from arithmetic and logic, of course the same phenomena turn up in ordinary scientific contexts. Given that we're out to know the world, some concepts suit this practice better than others; indeed, some concepts can lead us into conflict with the truth. Goodman's 'grue' is a particularly stark, artificial example – projecting 'grue' rather than 'green' will eventually lead us astray – but 'caloric', 'dephlogisticated air', 'light ether' and other standard examples from the history of science will also serve: if we formulate our theories in terms of these concepts and use them in our usual ways, we're led to false conclusions, indeed to false predictions. In pursuit of any inquiry, concepts can be better or worse, and some are outright wrong, just as 'tonk' is wrong in the practice of inference.

At this point, we should pause again to check in with the Second Philosopher. She's agreed with Wittgenstein that our meanings are fixed by a complex interaction of our interests and motivations, our natural inclinations, and very general features of the world, and now she's faced with his similarly based account of what makes for a good logical rule. Of course her account of logical truth has emphasized the role of 'very general features of the world', so on that score, her agreement clearly continues. As for our natural inclinations to infer one way rather than another, these she sees as rooted in our most basic cognitive machinery, presumably as a result of our (and our ancestors') experience with those very general features. But this isn't all; in fact, she takes the logical practices we have to be shaped by our interests and inclinations more directly. For comparison, consider natural science: the world has whatever structure it has, but what we notice, what we study depends on our aims – we care about physics, biology, botany for a range of different reasons – and our aptitudes – presumably some aspects of the world are closed to us, or at least quite difficult for us to fathom, because of our cognitive and physical limitations. If our goals and abilities were different, we might well be studying other features of the world from those we do in fact study. In these respects, logic is no different, so again the Second Philosopher is in broad agreement with Wittgenstein: our logical practices, too, rest on the same trio of interests and motivations, natural inclinations, and very general features of the world.

But now another niggling worry begins to surface. However we manage to fix the meanings of our words, could the correctness of our logical laws really rest on so shallow a footing as our interests and goals, our human nature, and general features of the physical world? The notion that logic is somehow special takes many forms, to some of which we now turn.

Chapter 6

But Isn't Logic Special?!

The most common objection to treating logic along the lines of rule-following in general is that this overlooks, or fails to fairly honor, some deep and distinctive feature of logic. Pears puts the point this way:

> The logical necessities that we recognize seem to be the indispensable conditions of all thought, like the air that we breathe, and we find it hard to imagine continuing to think without them. . . . the application of any general word might well have been different from what it now is, and it is often easy to imagine circumstances in which it really would have been different. . . . But logic seems to be made of harder stuff. (Pears [2006], p. 65)

Worries of this kind surface dramatically in Wittgenstein's metaphilosophical discussions of logic in the *Investigations*:

> In what way is logic something sublime? . . . Logical investigation explores the essence of all things. It seeks to see the foundation of things, and shouldn't concern itself whether things actually happen in this or that way. (*PI* §89)
>
> Our investigation is directed not toward *phenomena*, but rather, as one might say, toward the '*possibilities*' of phenomena. (*PI* §90)

A similar sentiment turns up early in Part I of the *Remarks*, continuing the passage quoted a few pages back, the one that begins with the interlocutor's protest that 'I must only infer what really *follows*!' and Wittgenstein's query 'only what follows, going by *such* rules of inference as somehow agree with some (sort of) reality?' To this point, we've taken the interlocutor to be raising a question about ordinary truth, ordinary reality, but now he ups the ante to something more:

> Here what is before our minds in a vague way is that this reality is something very abstract, very general, and very rigid. Logic is a kind of ultra-physics, the description of the 'logical structure' of the world, which we perceive through a kind of ultra-experience (with the understanding e.g.). (*RFM* I, §8)

Of course there's no missing the echoes of the *Tractatus* in this![1] One common contemporary version of this picture sees logical truth as special because it's metaphysically necessary, true in all possible worlds (and known, perhaps, by a kind of rational intuition).

Here we find a second instance of Wittgensteinian therapy. Imagine that our troubled philosopher from the previous chapter has overcome his demand for the priority of sense and come to appreciate the sufficiency of the ordinary practices of rule-following and the general facts on which they're based. Now he's asked to

1. I hope it's equally clear that despite the Second Philosopher's talk of 'the "logical structure" of the world' – though she would omit the scare quotes – it would take a considerable stretch to locate her position in this quotation. 'Very general' fits well, but 'very abstract' less so, and 'very rigid' is hard to interpret at all along second-philosophical lines. 'Ultra-physics' sounds stronger than merely more general than physics, and 'ultra-experience' or 'perceiv[ing] with the understanding' would be an odd way of describing the impression of obviousness that comes with the Second Philosopher's simple logical truths. In fact, the quotation seems intended to express a yearning for something more than the Second Philosopher's ordinary truths about the world.

regard logical inference as similarly based, and he balks on the grounds that logical truth is necessary, so it can't arise from the contingent 'grey rags and dust' of rule-following. As long as the demand for necessity is in place, there's no need even to examine the details and contexts of our inferential practices. So Wittgenstein's therapeutic job is to unseat this demand.

He attempts to do this in *RFM*, Part I, by introducing a second line of thought largely[2] absent from the *Investigations*: consideration of odd practices quite different from our own, designed to show that our ways of doing things aren't the only ways. If he succeeds in this, the idea that logic is 'true in all possible worlds' may lose its force. I propose to focus on two contrasting examples: the rubber rulers and the odd nut-sharer.

First, the rubber rulers:

> How should we get into conflict with the truth, if our footrules were made of very soft rubber instead of wood and or steel? . . . A shopkeeper might use [such a ruler] to treat different customers differently.
>
> If a ruler expanded to an extraordinary extent when slightly heated, we should say – in normal circumstances – that that made it *unusable*. But we could think of a situation in which this was just what was wanted. (*RFM* I, §5)

Here the interlocutor protests – 'But surely that isn't measuring at all!' – and is reminded:

> It is similar to our measuring and capable, in certain circumstances, of fulfilling 'practical purposes'. (*RFM*, I, §5)

2. The only exception I know of is the growing and shrinking lumps of cheese noted above (*PI* §142). I come back to this case below.

This wouldn't be what we call 'measuring', but it might well be a sustainable practice, even for us, if, for example, we were particularly keen on allowing shopkeepers to treat different customers differently. In the original rule-following example, a single wayward student appears in our midst, and the question is how to justify our conviction that for '+ 2' as we all understand it, 1004 is wrong and 1002 is right. Now we're presented with a free-standing alternative practice with a different concept in place of our 'measurement', but the measurement-like concept of this practice is also supported, as is ours, by the practitioners' common interests, sense of salience, natural reactions, and so on.[3]

Compare this with the case of the odd nut-sharer:

> Imagine someone bewitched so that he calculated
>
> 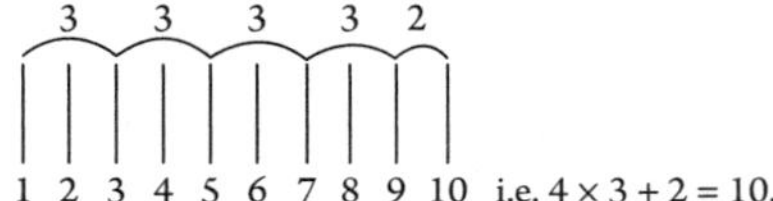
>
>
> Now he is to apply this calculation. He takes 3 nuts four times over, and then 2 more, and he divides them among 10 people and each one gets *one* nut; for he shares them out in a way corresponding to the loops of the calculation, and as often as he gives someone a second nut it disappears. (*RFM* I, §137)

Here it isn't the calculator's interests, or natural reactions, or classifications that are at issue: though his calculation looks wrong to

3. The wood-sellers of *RFM* I, §§149–150, are similar, though perhaps a bit more distant from ourselves. See Stroud [1965].

us, if he calculated as we do in the world he lives in, he would 'come into conflict with the truth'; if he calculated as we do, and tried to distribute three nuts to each of four people, he'd find the twelve nuts he thought adequate in fact wouldn't be enough. (The second nut he hands to each person would disappear, so he'd have to give each of them four nuts, not three.) In this case, what's odd isn't human interests or human nature, but the world itself.

Still, as the cheese-weighing example[4] shows, this theme – the idea that different practices might be natural if the world were different – isn't peculiar to the *Remarks*. In the *Investigations*, Wittgenstein appends this note to the cheese case:

> What we have to mention in order to explain the significance, I mean the importance, of a concept are often extremely general facts of nature: such facts as are hardly ever mentioned because of their great generality. (Note after *PI* §142)

In 'Philosophy of Psychology — A Fragment' (formerly published as Part II of the *Philosophical Investigations*),[5] he elaborates:

4. To recall: 'The procedure of putting a lump of cheese on a balance and fixing the price by the turn of the scale would lose its point if it frequently happened that such lumps suddenly grew or shrank with no obvious cause' (*PI* §142).
5. Here it must be admitted that *PPF* cannot be regarded as comparable in authority to *PI*, Part I. Stern [2004], p. 2, describes the situation this way: 'the final typescript of Part I was produced in the mid–1940s. . . . Wittgenstein continued to work on related topics, and it is likely that if his life had not been cut short in 1951 . . . he would have worked some of that material into the end of that typescript. As a result, his trustees decided to include a rearrangement of the most polished work from the second half of the 1940s in the *Philosophical Investigations*, and to call it 'Part II'. However, what we now have as 'Part I' is the final version of the book that Wittgenstein worked on during the second half of his philosophical career. For that reason [it] has a very different status from the rest of his posthumous publications'. (See Wittgenstein [1953], pp. xxi–xxiii, for details.) Given that this material is 'the most polished' of the later work on the philosophy of psychology – it 'consists of carefully selected excerpts . . . originally gathered as readings for Norman Malcolm and his students when visiting Cornell in 1948' (Stern [2004], p. 167) – I treat it as on a par with Part I of *RFM*.

> If anyone believes that certain concepts are absolutely the correct ones, and that having different ones would mean not realizing something that we realize – then let him imagine certain very general facts of nature to be different from what we are used to, and the formation of concepts different from the usual ones will become intelligible to him. (*PPF* §366)

Here again, the rule-following morals are clear: the viability of our practices rests on our interests, our natures, *and* the way the world is. Contemplation of these odd examples opens our eyes to the ways different interests (the rubber rulers) or different physical realities (the nut-sharer) could produce equally well-supported practices that are quite alien to ours. Presumably the same could be said for natural reactions; for example, we've noted (in the previous chapter) that a group of people might find it natural to continue '+ 2' as the wayward student does, and still pursue something very like our arithmetic.

How is all this intended to help our troubled philosopher? We're now asking him to imagine a practice driven by different interests, shaped by different perceptions of what's natural, or formed in a physical world quite different from our own – and in which our logic would be inappropriate and perhaps another logic appropriate. To take an example of differing interests, the practice of writing one statement after another might be intended to generate pleasing wallpaper patterns[6] rather than transitions from truths to truths; or, for an example of a different sense of naturalness, consider a community that finds it unnatural to extend a chain of inference beyond three steps. In either case, it's not surprising that

6. I didn't make this up. In one of the later passages of the *Remarks*, selected by the editors, Wittgenstein writes: 'imagine equations used as ornaments (wallpaper patterns)' (*RFM* VII, §40).

a different 'logic' might emerge, but these possibilities wouldn't shake our philosopher's conviction that the laws of logic are in fact necessarily true for all that. For his purposes, the crucial case is the nut-sharers.

Assuming that elementary arithmetic is just a variant of rudimentary logic,[7] the nut-sharer case not only involves a difference in the objective features of the world – as does the cheese-weighing case from *PI* – it reaches deep into the KF-structure of the world. It isn't clear from the brief description whether the nut-sharer's world falls short of full KF-structure or enjoys a KF-structure too fleeting and unstable to be of practical use, but either way, we see Wittgenstein gesturing toward the very structures the Second Philosopher has identified as the ground of logical truth. Predictably, in the nut-sharer's world, our ways of calculating would go wrong – and if our world were more like his, we might do well to calculate as he does, just as we might do well to forgo the distributive law if the macro-world behaved more like the quantum world. If meditating on the nut-sharers or the mysteries of quantum mechanics are enough to persuade our troubled philosopher that logic would fail in sufficiently strange circumstances, then the way is open to his acknowledging that logic is just one case in the general account of rule-following.[8]

If Wittgenstein and his second-philosophical ally are right about the contingency of logical truth, then one kind of supposed

7. As does the Second Philosopher (see [2007], pp. 318–319, [2014]), and apparently also Wittgenstein: '"But doesn't it follow with logical necessity that you get two when you add one to one, and three when you add one to two?, and isn't this inexorability the same as that of logical inference?" – Yes! it is the same.' (*RFM* I, §5).

8. Something odd has happened here, methodologically speaking: it's hard to see how Wittgenstein's therapeutic treatment of the troubled philosopher's belief that logical truth is necessary differs in kind (or even in spirit) from the Second Philosopher's direct argument that logic is contingent. I come back to this question in footnotes 6 and 8 of chapter 7.

specialness that logic might enjoy – truth in all possible worlds – has been debunked. But logic is sometimes thought to be distinctive in another, less dramatic way, an example of which might be found in Frege's thinking on the subject.[9] Every science has its laws, its principles, that inquirers must follow, to use Frege's apt phrase, 'if they are not to miss the truth' (Frege [1897], p. 250):

> Any law that states what is can be conceived as prescribing that one should think in accordance with it. . . . This holds for geometrical and physical laws no less than for logical laws. (Frege [1897], p. 202)

What sets logical laws apart, he continues, is simply

> that they are the most general laws, which prescribe universally how one should think if one is to think at all. (Frege [1893], p. 202)

On this picture, we might say that the laws of biology are binding *if one wishes to understand the physical structure, origins, and life cycles of living organisms*; the laws of chemistry are binding *if one wishes to understand the composition, properties, and reactions of substances*; but the laws of logic are binding on any inquiry whatsoever. Though the other sciences pursue truth, and thus can come into conflict with it, logic's relationship to the truth is special:

9. I don't mean to endorse any particular interpretive claims about Frege's views in this brief passage. My goal is just to use Frege's writings, and some aspects of Burge's reading of them (in the essays of his [2005]), as a path toward isolating another way (other than necessity) that logic might be thought to be special. See also MacFarlane [2002].

> To discover truths is the task of all sciences; it falls to logic to discern the laws of truth. (Frege [1918/1919], p. 325)

The various natural laws concern the truths of some aspect X of the world, where X might be the world's biological or chemical features, but logical laws are binding on all our investigations; they are unconditional, the laws of truth tout court.

Now this could be understood simply as saying that logical laws are the most general, not that they differ in kind from other scientific laws; this would be a version of the position our troubled philosopher is out to resist. To preserve the distinctiveness of logic, he might be inclined at this point to fall back on metaphysical necessity: the laws of logic are unconditional because they hold in all possible worlds. But, at least on Tyler Burge's reading, this doesn't appear to be what Frege has in mind:

> Modal categories are surprisingly absent from Frege's discussion . . . (Burge [2000], p. 367) . . . Frege seems to avoid invocation of an independent modal notion of modality . . . in epistemology, metaphysics, and logic. (Burge [2000], p. 370)

The troubled philosopher's appeal to necessity is obviously absent here: who knows or cares what goes on in other possible worlds, but in our world, logical laws, unlike biological or botanical or chemical laws, apply to absolutely every area of inquiry; so logic is special, not because its laws are true in all possible worlds, but because they're true in application to absolutely every aspect of our world. But again, if we're out to preserve the distinctiveness of logic, we need more than this. The idea must be that logic holds everywhere somehow *in principle*, not simply as a matter of accidental fact. And finally, presumably, this must be something we know a priori.[10]

Questions naturally arise about what kind of fact this is and how we come to know it in this special way. Frege's answer, according to Burge, is a subtle and innovative version of rationalism, the idea that our a priori knowledge of objective logical truth is gained by Reason.[11] Kant also has an answer that rests on his transcendental idealism: who knows what the world is like in itself, or how God (an intuitive intellect) would see it, but the world *we* experience must obey the laws of logic, and we know this a priori, because our world is partly constituted by the forms of judgment and pure categories.[12] Setting rationalism and idealism aside, though, our concern here is with Wittgenstein. I see no hint of Wittgenstein doubting that the laws of logic apply in all our investigations of the world – which of course opens some daylight between him and the Second Philosopher – but for now the question is whether or not he thinks there's something 'in principle', perhaps some special a priori knowledge, involved in the universality of logic.

Some evidence for the affirmative comes in the way he connects logic to his elusive category of the 'grammatical'. Recall the interlocutor's insistence on truth:

> 'But I can infer only what actually does follow.' (*RFM* I, §119)

10. As we've seen (in chapter 2), the Second Philosopher may have room for a limited form of a priori knowledge of rudimentary logic: since the validity of these logical laws arises from our fundamental cognitive capacities, the simpler cases will appear obvious to us, so we might be said to believe them a priori. A sufficiently externalist epistemology might hold that this amounts to a priori knowledge, because the evolutionary and maturational processes that generate those capacities are reliable. Even if this sort of line can be filled in, it isn't the sort of thing we're looking for: presumably the 'in principle' universality of logic is supposed to be accessible to us without empirical investigation.
11. See Burge [2005], the introduction and Part III. (Part III includes Burge [2000], cited above.)
12. Recall footnote 7 of chapter 1.

Now she could mean nothing more by this than what the Second Philosopher would – 'I have to obey the laws of rudimentary logic if I'm to successfully describe the world's KF-structures, such as they are' – but, as we've seen, the Wittgensteinian response leaps over this modest idea and saddles the defenseless interlocutor with a version of the sublimity of logic:

> – That is to say: what the logical machine really does produce. The logical machine – that would be an all-pervading ethereal mechanism. (*RFM* I, §119)

And, naturally, this meets with disapproval:

> – We must give warning against this picture. (*RFM* I, §119)

The warning takes the form of a few pages on the notion of a 'rigid' machine and the hardness of the logical must, some of it overlapping §§191–197 of the *Investigations*, and then we get:

> The connexion which is not supposed to be a causal, experiential one, but much stricter and harder, so rigid even, that the one thing somehow already *is* the other, is always a connexion in grammar. (*RFM* I, §128)

Though Wittgenstein rejects the usual claim of metaphysical necessity, he appears to be suggesting that some 'grammatical' kernel is what inspires the troubled philosopher's move to the sublime. Of course this can't be ordinary grammar, as understood by either the schoolteacher or the linguist, so the question of what this actually comes to remains to be explored.

This notion of a grammatical proposition or a grammatical connection appears in the *Investigations* as well, not as applied strictly to logical truth, but more generally to anything the troubled philosopher is tempted to count as necessary:

> What does it mean when we say, 'I can't imagine the opposite of this' . . . We use these words to fend off something whose form produces an illusion of being an empirical proposition, but which is really a grammatical one. (*PI* §251)

The contrast with ordinary contingent claims is repeated:

> The analysis oscillates between natural science and grammar. (*PI* §392)

But to classify a claim as grammatical isn't to say that it's arbitrary. The interlocutor conveniently makes this mistake:

> 'So does what is, and what is not, called (logically) possible depend wholly on our grammar – that is, on what that permits?' – But surely that is arbitrary! (*PI* §520)

The response:

> Is it arbitrary? – It is not every sentence-like formation that we know how to do something with, not every technique that has a use in our life. (*PI* §520)[13]

13. Cf. *RFM* I, §116: '. . . inferring . . . is of course bounded for us, not by an arbitrary definition, but by natural limits corresponding to the body of what can be called the role of . . . inferring in our life.'

At this point, we've circled back to grounding our practice of logical inference in the various contingent features of our interests, our nature, and general facts about the world. And once again it becomes difficult so see what makes logic special, as opposed to our practices of biology, botany, physics, chemistry and the rest.

So what, if anything, *does* make grammar in general, and logic in particular, special? All I have to offer is this passage from Part I of the *Remarks*:

> Isn't it like this: so long as one thinks it can't be otherwise, one draws logical conclusions. This presumably means: so long as *such-and-such is not brought in question at all.*
>
> The steps that are not brought in question are logical inferences. But the reason why they are not brought in question is not that they 'certainly correspond to the truth' – or something of the sort, – no, it is just this that is called 'thinking', 'speaking', 'inferring', 'arguing'. There is not any question at all here of some correspondence between what is said and reality; rather is logic *antecedent* to any such correspondence; in the same sense, that is, as that in which the establishment of a method of measurement is *antecedent* to the correctness or incorrectness of a statement of length. (*RFM* I, §156)

It's tempting to read this as saying that, yes, all our practices are based on these various contingent, general facts, but some parts of those practices are, in a sense, constitutive ('antecedent'); that is, these must be in place for the practice of getting things right and wrong ('corresponding to the truth') to get off the ground; we can tell which parts these are because they are in fact never called into question; and finally, logical laws are among these. In this way,

Wittgenstein might hold at once that logic is contingent, that logic applies to absolutely everything because it is constitutive of our practice in the most general sense, that it is prior to all justification, and thus that it neither needs nor admits of justification itself. Logic would be special for us in this way, in our world, despite there being alternatives.

In fact, a reading along these lines can be found in Hacker.[14] After highlighting precisely the same passage (*RFM* I, §156), he parses it this way:

> Both Platonism and psychologism err in holding that the laws of thinking are *correct*, and owe their correctness to something extraneous to them, i.e. to the laws of truth . . . (Frege) or to the workings of the human mind (psychologism). Wittgenstein argued that rules of inference are autonomous. They are neither correct nor incorrect. Rather they are constitutive of reasoning, thinking, inferring. (Baker and Hacker [2009], p. 320)

This roughly Kantian idea, that logic is constitutive of inquiry, and therefore immune to confirmation or disconfirmation, can also be found in recent interpretations of Carnap's linguistic frameworks: a framework (with its logic) provides the setting necessary for any meaningful inquiry; the only cognitively significant questions are those posed within a framework.[15] In the terminology of the late Wittgenstein, perhaps it's fair to see our practice as a language game, and if meaning is roughly determined by use in such a game, then the suggestion is that the 'grammar' of the game

14. See Baker and Hacker [2009], §VII.9. I attribute this position to Hacker alone, because after co-authoring the first edition (1985), Baker took a quite different, almost literally therapeutic line (see Baker [2004]), and the second edition (2009) was then extensively revised by Hacker.
15. See [2007], §I.5, especially pp. 69–70.

(which includes logic) must be in place before meaningful inquiry can begin.

The trouble with this reading is that it looks unsettlingly like a revival of something in the vicinity of the priority of sense: the rules of the language game have to be in place before anything can be compared to the world. Whatever the appeal of this neo-Kantian or proto-Carnapian idea, I think we should hesitate to attribute it to the late Wittgenstein. It's clear that Wittgenstein was continually tempted by philosophical views he was also at pains to reject, which suggests another way of reading the key passage from at *RFM* I, §156. To get an idea of how this would go, let's return for a moment to the treatment of rule-following, in particular to Saul Kripke's reading and its shortcomings. First a bit of stage-setting...

Faced with the many questions and responses, quotations and replies that make up the text of the *Investigations*, I've been following the common approach of isolating one strand as 'the interlocutor', the figure proposing various philosophical theories, often the same as the figure I've been calling the 'troubled philosopher'. But there's also the voice who responds to the interlocutor, the one who offers the idea that meaning is use, or that following a rule is a practice. David Stern, following Stanley Cavell, calls these 'the voice of temptation' and 'the voice of correctness', respectively:

> The 'voice of temptation' ... begins to formulate various philosophical theories, and the 'voice of correctness' . . . replies to these theories. (Stern [2004], p. 74)

> [The voice of correctness] is usually taken to be arguing for Wittgenstein's own philosophical position ... while [the voice of temptation] attacks ..., arguing that it does not do justice to his intuitions and his arguments. (Stern [2004], p. 24)

> [At various points], the [voice of correctness] is . . . used to set out behaviourist, verificationist, and anti-essentialist objections to traditional philosophical views, in opposition to [the voice of temptation] that expressed mentalist, verification-transcendent, and essentialist intuitions and convictions. (Stern [2004], p. 22)[16]

The key observation, common to Stern and Cavell, is that neither of these voices represents Wittgenstein's position. There is, in addition, a third voice, that of a third figure Stern calls 'the commentator'.

The commentator's job, Wittgenstein's job, is to take potshots at both sides, to provide

> . . . a commentary consisting partly of objections to assumptions the debaters take for granted, and partly of platitudes about language and everyday life they have both overlooked. (Stern [2004], p. 22)

Notice that this can be seen as a double-barreled version of the simpler therapeutic model employed earlier: before we saw Wittgenstein as offering ordinary answers to questions about how we follow rules or draw logical inferences (the gray rags and dust), then uncovering and debunking the unnoticed presupposition that keeps the troubled philosopher from appreciating the force of these ordinary answers (the priority of sense, the necessity of logic). Stern's observations point toward more complicated cases, where two philosophers disagree sharply, both of them undervaluing the ordinary

16. Notice that the voice of correctness takes different positions at different times, depending on what's being expressed by the voice of temptation.

answers, and Wittgenstein aims to show that the debate itself rests on an unexamined presupposition that they share.

Applying this more complex construction to the case of rule-following, we find the voice of temptation attempting to provide a 'straight solution' to the purported paradox, in terms of images or meanings or intentions or whatever, and the voice of correctness attempting to provide a 'skeptical solution', as Kripke does, in terms of shared practices. Stern argues that:

> The 'straight' and the 'sceptical' solutions are equally misguided, for they both misunderstand the character and methods of the *Philosophical Investigations*. They mistakenly identify the viewpoint defended in a particular strand of the argument . . . as equivalent to the views that are advocated by the author, or by the book as a whole. (Stern [2004], p. 23)

Kripke, on this reading, does just this, taking the voice of correctness for Wittgenstein's own, seeing Wittgenstein as 'setting out his own . . . philosophical position on the topic of rule-following', seeing his own task

> as a matter of extracting and refining [Wittgenstein's] philosophical theory from the admittedly unconventional exposition he provides. (Stern [2004], p. 152)

Stern's alternative is that Wittgenstein himself eschews theorizing of both varieties, in favor of an appreciation of the grey rags and dust; when we attend to our ordinary practices with unbiased eyes, we recognize that there is no paradox. In the previous chapter, the interlocutor's blindness to the plain facts of rule-following was traced to the pull of the priority of sense, to the imagined need for a type of meaning that determines correct and incorrect uses not just in fact but in any possible circumstance. We now see that the same imagined need lies in the background when the voice of correctness takes the paradox seriously. The same preconception, the same false worry, inspires both the straight and the skeptical responses.

Returning now to the case of logic, we've been asking whether there's any evidence that Wittgenstein took logical laws to be universal in some principled way, and we turned to his discussion of 'grammar' as the best hope of a positive answer. Given that the 'logic is grammar' line certainly presents a controversial philosophical thesis, given also that it echoes a view that apparently continued to tempt Wittgenstein, it seems most likely that a passage like *Remarks* I, §156 – about logic being 'antecedent' – would have ended up in the voice of correctness, had Wittgenstein reworked and developed this material to his satisfaction. The related passages in the *Investigations* do seem to bear this sort of interpretation. Speaking of 'grammar' in another connection, Stern writes:

> On Hacker's reading, Wittgenstein appeals to the grammar of our language to show that what philosophers say makes no sense. While it is true that there is a strand in the book's dialogue – Cavell's 'voice of correctness' – that does make use of grammar in just this way, I take it that the point of the book is not to get us to cheer on this side of the debate. Rather, to say that philosophy is nonsense is just to say that it falls apart when we try to make sense of it. . . . But this must emerge out of the reader's involvement in the dialogue of the *Philosophical Investigations,* our being tempted into particular philosophical theories, and our coming to see that those particular attempts at theorizing are nonsensical, rather than a more general

> principle, or overarching method, that any one voice in the dialogue is advocating. (Stern [2004], p. 83)

In our case, the voice of temptation insists that logical truth is metaphysically necessary, and the voice of correctness replies that what appears to be necessary is really just grammatical, constitutive of inquiry. In the rule-following case, Wittgenstein himself rests with the mundane observation that 'we are not on tenterhooks about what [the rule] will tell us next, but it always tells us the same, and we do what it tells us' (*PI* §223); the rule-follower says, 'This is simply what I do' (*PI* §217). The counterpart for logic was quoted above: the logical steps are 'the ones that are not called in question' (*RFM* I, §152).

So it appears Wittgenstein and the Second Philosopher can agree that logic isn't special in either of the senses we've considered (necessary or 'grammatical'), that logical inference is simply a sort of rule-following, that our ordinary explanations and responses work perfectly well, and that the viability of these practices rests on our shared interests, natural human responses, and very general features of the world. Both can agree with the logic-is-special theorist that the reliability of logic doesn't depend on how we happen to classify things or on the details of the world's regularities, but it still does depend on there being ordinary properties and relations that classify things, not to mention stable things themselves to classify. So it isn't that logic doesn't depend on contingent features of the world, but that the structures it depends on are so simple, so ubiquitous, so obvious as to be nearly invisible:

> We are, indeed, . . . interested in the correspondence between concepts and very general facts of nature. . . . Such facts as mostly do not strike us because of their generality. (*PPF*, §365)

These general facts are, of course, the facts of KF-structuring – so usual, so natural that we find it hard to imagine them failing. Both Wittgenstein and the Second Philosopher work by turning our attention to odd cases where they just might fail.[17] So logic depends on worldly structure just as the other sciences do; the impression otherwise arises only because the structures it depends on are *the* most general, and therefore *the* most unremarkable and unnoticed.[18]

It apparently didn't occur to Wittgenstein that some corner of our world might be too recalcitrant to support this practice, as the Second Philosopher suspects of the micro-world, but the example of the nut-sharer suggests that he wouldn't reject the possibility out of hand.[19] At this point, then, any remaining disagreement between them is a straightforward empirical matter of the facts of quantum mechanics, to be resolved by the methods of physics.

17. See footnote 8.

18. As we might put it, Wittgenstein and the Second Philosopher agree that what's wrong with 'tonk' and 'affirming the consequent' is no different in kind from what's wrong with Buster's house; our practices of inferring and house-building both rest on our interests, our natural inclinations and abilities, and general facts about the world.

19. He does ask, in the margin: 'Are our laws of inference eternal and immutable?' (*RFM* I, §155).

Chapter 7

Naturalizing the Logical Must

If the empirical question just noted were his only unresolved issue with the Second Philosopher, then the late Wittgenstein's position on logic would already be naturalistic, in need of no further tweak. The practice of logic, for both, would rest on a complex combination of our interests and motivations, our natural responses, and those 'very general facts of nature' (*PPF* §365). The Second Philosopher's contribution would simply be to fill in some of the specifics: given our interest in and motivations for describing the world, logic is reliable insofar as the world has this very general KF-structuring, and our natural responses play the role they do because our basic cognitive mechanisms are tuned to detecting those structures; she goes on to spell out the details of these claims and to marshal empirical evidence in their support. The two positions would be entirely compatible.

But, as it happens, this *isn't* the only unresolved issue between Wittgenstein and the Second Philosopher, because, as we've seen, Wittgenstein rejects all explanation, all justification and all theorizing. Of course the rule-follower's own explanations and justifications will eventually come to an end, as in the passage noted a moment ago:

> Once I have exhausted the justifications [for my acting in *this* way – e.g., saying 1002, not 1004], I have reached bedrock, and

> my spade is turned. Then I am inclined to say: 'This is simply what I do'. (*PI* §217)

In the logic case, if someone asks why I'm justified in concluding that it's green, given that it's either red or green and it's not red, there are things I can say – 'look here, there are only two possibilities, don't you see? and one of them is ruled out' – but in the end, if my conversation partner doesn't get the point, I have nothing more to offer. On these observations about the kinds of justifications open to the ordinary rule-follower, Wittgenstein and the Second Philosopher agree, but the point at issue now is what's open to the philosopher, to the observer of, the commentator on, these various behaviors, and here Wittgenstein insists that

> we may not advance any kind of theory . . . all *explanation* must disappear. (*PI* §109).
>
> Philosophy must . . . in the end only describe [the actual use of language] . . . It cannot . . . justify it. (*PI* §124)
>
> Philosophy . . . neither explains nor deduces anything. (*PI* §126)

The irrelevance of empirical inquiry like the Second Philosopher's is sometimes quite explicit:

> Our considerations must not be scientific ones. (*PI* §109)
>
> Above all, don't wonder 'What might be going on in the eyes or brain here?' (*PPF* §243)[1]

1. See also *RPP*, volume 1, §§903–909, or *Zettel*, §§608–613, discussed below.

At this point, obviously, Wittgenstein and the Second Philosopher part company. Her scientific inquiries can't be viewed as filling in Wittgenstein's picture, after all, because his is a picture that cannot, for whatever reason, be elaborated empirically.

So what is the reason, why *does* Wittgenstein take this stand? One commentator who's struggled mightily with this very question is David Pears; it runs through all four of his books on Wittgenstein's philosophy (Pears [1969], [1987], [1988], [2006]). In *The False Prison,* he quotes *PPF* §§365–366 – of which we've so far seen only glimpses – this time in full:[2]

> If concept formation can be explained by facts of nature, shouldn't we be interested, not in grammar, but rather in what is its basis in nature? – We are, indeed, also interested in the correspondence between concepts and very general facts of nature. (Such facts as mostly do not strike us because of their generality.) But our interest is not thereby thrown back on to these possible causes of concept formation; we are not doing natural science; nor yet natural history – since we can also invent fictitious natural history for our purposes. (*PPF* §365)
>
> I am not saying: if such-and-such facts of nature were different, people would have different concepts (in the sense of a hypothesis). Rather: if anyone believes that certain concepts are absolutely the correct ones, and that having different ones would mean not realizing something we realize – then let him imagine certain very general facts of nature to be different from what we are used to, and the formation of concepts different from the usual ones will become intelligible to him. (*PPF* §366)

2. Pears [1988], p. 450. Pears uses the older translation; I've updated to the fourth edition of *PI* and *PPF*.

Pears' response to this is strikingly second-philosophical in tone:

> How can his appeal to the naturalness of certain practices stop short of an investigation of what makes them natural? Maybe his [interest is not . . . thrown back on to these possible causes of concept formation],[3] but if language has grown out of a pre-linguistic pattern of discriminations that is locked into our environment in complex ways, how can the philosophical study of language avoid including this part of its natural history? (Pears [1988], p. 451)
>
> The point at which there is pressure on him to expand the scope of his philosophy and include facts of a different kind has . . . been located. It is the point at which the speaker's reasons for saying what he does say run out, and he can only tell us that this is the way in which he finds it natural to go on. Why not try to explain its naturalness instead of leaving it to the speaker to do the only thing that he can do, namely report it as a matter of phenomenological fact? (Pears [1988], p. 515)

In the conclusion to his earliest book, Pears identifies this tension as one of Wittgenstein's greatest strengths:

> It is only half of the truth to say that his resistance to science produced his later view of philosophy. There was also his linguistic naturalism,[4] which played an equally important role. These two tendencies . . . are not diametrically opposed to one

3. Here again I amend to the most recent translation of *PPF*, §365.

4. Pears introduces this term by analogy with Hume: Hume's 'philosophy is a kind of psychological naturalism. Wittgenstein's later philosophy is another species in the same genus: it is not psychological naturalism, but linguistic naturalism' (Pears [1969], p. 184). The similarities and dissimilarities are further traced in his [1988], pp. 513–515. Though I won't attempt to lay out this line of thought here, it is the one that eventually leads Pears to conclude that 'the spirit in which Wittgenstein records his facts [of actual

> another. But there is a great tension between them, and his later philosophy is an expression of this tension. Each of the two forces without the other would have produced results of much less interest. The linguistic naturalism by itself would have been a dreary kind of philosophy done under a low and leaden sky. The resistance to science by itself might have led to almost any kind of nonsense. But together they produced something truly great. (Pears [1969], pp. 197–198)

By the time of his final interpretive contribution, he seems less confident, suggesting that 'this deeply anti-theoretical philosophy' might be

> misguided . . . because his ideas about meaning are too restrictive and because the point at which he saw his opponent's theories vanish in the void of meaninglessness was too near home. (Pears [2006], p. x)

Harkening back to the early book, he writes that the new one

> is written with the same conviction that the structure of Wittgenstein's ideas and the connections between them owe much to an imagination that is essential to philosophy but can so very easily lead us nowhere. (Pears [2006], p. x)

Of course the Second Philosopher is content to carry out her inquiries under a version of that naturalistic 'low and leaden sky'.

---

language use] does make it difficult for him to maintain the purity of philosophy as he conceives it' [i.e., its independence of science] (Pears [1988], p. 515). This comes at the beginning of the paragraph that ends with the question, quoted above, 'why not try to explain its naturalness?.'

Now there's no doubting, as a matter of biographical fact, Wittgenstein's 'contempt for scientism' (Pears [1988], p. 221), 'his strong feeling that the great danger to which modern thought is exposed is domination by science' (Pears [1969], p. 197). The biographer Ray Monk records the Spenglarian gloom of remarks like these:

> I was walking about in Cambridge and passed a bookshop, and in the window were portraits of Russell, Freud and Einstein. A little further on, in a music shop, I saw portraits of Beethoven, Schubert and Chopin. Comparing these portraits I felt intensely the terrible degeneration that had come over the human spirit in the course of only a hundred years. (quoted in Monk [1990], p. 299, from Drury's recollections in Rhees [1984], p. 112)

> It isn't absurd, e.g., to believe that the age of science and technology is the beginning of the end for humanity; that the idea of great progress is a delusion, along with the idea that the truth will ultimately be known; that there is nothing good or desirable about scientific knowledge and that mankind, in seeking it, is falling into a trap. It is by no means obvious that this is not how things are. (quoted in Monk [1990], p. 485, from Wittgenstein [1980], p. 56e)

Monk concludes that 'the darkness of this time', a phrase from Wittgenstein's preface to the *Investigations* (p. 43),

> is directly attributable to the worship of the false idol of science against which his own work had been directed since the early 1930s. (Monk [1990], p. 486)

Though the Second Philosopher can't be said to worship at any altar, she certainly does practice the very methods that others (purportedly) falsely idolize.

Despite the obvious passion of Wittgenstein's personal distaste for science, this by itself presents no obstacle to the Second Philosopher's efforts to bring empirical findings to bear. To get beyond the merely psychological, we need to ask two questions: what *philosophical* reasons does Wittgenstein have for excluding science from his inquiries? are these good reasons, that is, for our purposes, reasons that present a challenge to the Second Philosopher? As it happens, those principled reasons aren't so easy to identify, so let's begin with the first question, intermingling discussion of the second as we go along.

One approach is to take Wittgenstein as holding that his therapeutic philosophizing is all there is to the subject:[5] there are no genuine philosophical problems; all apparent philosophical problems are generated by misunderstandings and mistaken preconceptions; the only genuine philosophical activity is to treat troubled philosophers, to help them free themselves from these merely apparent perplexities by straightforward description of obvious facts.[6] In Pears' words:

5. In [2011a], I suggest that some of Austin's work can be understood on a therapeutic model, but when he speaks of 'a technique for dissolving philosophical worries', he immediately adds, '*some* kinds of philosophical worry, not the whole of philosophy' ([1962], p. 5).

6. This way of putting things downplays the part about uncovering and debunking the unexamined assumption that keeps the troubled philosopher from appreciating the force of the ordinary answers – and it's this part of the 'treatment' that can start to look very much like a garden-variety piece of philosophical argumentation (see footnotes 8 and 17 of chapter 6). Notice that Stroud's therapeutic reading of the private language argument (sketched in footnote 6 of chapter 5) doesn't appear to suffer from this difficulty, nor does Austin's 'treatment' of Ayer in his [1962]. ([2011a] gives a slightly different take on how Austin's therapeutic efforts might be more pure than Wittgenstein's.) See also the next two footnotes.

> The description is intended to make us see how our own linguistic devices work, simply by putting them in their place in our lives without using any technical terms. If we object, that nothing so familiar or banal can possibly yield philosophical understanding, he will reply that, on the contrary, it gives us all the insight that we need, and that the attempt to go beyond it and theorize can only produce misunderstanding. We think that we need nourishment when what we really need is clear water. (Pears [1988], pp. 218–219)

From this point of view, no science could be relevant. The apparent problem is produced by a misunderstanding of the obvious, so only a more careful look at what we already know can serve to undo it.

In our case of logical truth, this line of thought would unfold in two steps.[7] First, the troubled philosopher is confused about rule-following because he insists on the priority of sense; he's cured when attention to our ordinary rule-following practices reveals that they adequately support attributions of correctness and incorrectness entirely on their own. Second, the troubled philosopher is confused about logical truth because he insists that it must be special in some way, not simply one among many cases of rule-following; he's cured when attention to our ordinary inferential practices reveals that they adequately support the logical must. This would be the end of the story; the troubled philosopher is free of his perplexities.

But how odd this looks from the Second Philosopher's perspective! She never embraced the priority of sense or the specialness of

7. Again, to make this as plausible as possible, I've suppressed the 'uncovering and debunking' stage (see footnotes 6 and 8). For simplicity, I also ignore the 'voice of correctness' who responds to the 'voice of temptation' (our 'troubled philosopher) with a Kripkean 'skeptical solution' or a theory of grammaticality.

logical truth in the first place; she never demanded that a person following a rule or drawing an inference be able to offer more than the most mundane justifications for those actions. Nevertheless, she *does* want to know, among other things, what makes our logic so natural and so reliable, and she offers a stretch of empirical theory to answer these questions. In an analogous context, Pears protests:

> We certainly do not want to saddle [Wittgenstein] with the thesis that someone who asks, 'what is a number?' must already by confusing the abstract with the concrete. (Pears [1988], p. 218)

In cases like this, he writes:

> It is almost impossible to understand what is going on without transcending the resources available to someone engaged in the language game, so there is a strong case for extending the scope of his naturalism and including any facts about our lives that help us to understand our own systems of thought. (Pears [1988], p. 516)

Of course, the Second Philosopher would agree: the evidence available to her investigation of our inferential practices shouldn't be subjected to an artificial limit.[8]

One possible Wittgensteinian rejoinder at this point is to allow that the Second Philosopher's efforts may be in some way illuminating or worthwhile, but to deny that they qualify as philosophy.

8. Pears's own account of Wittgenstein's philosophical method may be more lenient than the austere therapy considered here; in particular, the 'critical phase' of philosophizing that he attributes to Wittgenstein (e.g., in the preface to his [2006]) might include the sort of uncovering and debunking that's passed over here in silence (see the two previous footnotes). This wouldn't alter the ultimate complaint, that an artificial limitation is being placed on philosophical inquiry.

This would be a largely terminological matter, and we might perhaps be forgiven for wondering how else to classify a serious attempt to answer the Second Philosopher's question, 'if it's red or green, and it's not red, why must it be green?', or more generally, 'what is the nature of logical truth?'. Questions like these, traditionally understood as 'philosophical', would remain open after Wittgenstein's therapeutic efforts were complete, and the Second Philosopher's attempts to answer them would remain legitimate. But, of course there's no point arguing about a label. Our interest here is in the possibility of more substantive grounds for Wittgenstein's prohibition against appeals to science, grounds that would rule out, not simply relabel, the Second Philosopher's inquiry. For a sense of what these grounds might be, let's consider three proposals offered by commentators.

The first of these appeals to some notorious remarks from Wittgenstein's less authoritative writings:

> No supposition seems to me more natural than that there is no process in the brain correlated with . . . thinking. (*RPP* §903, *Zettel* §608) It is . . . perfectly possible that certain psychological phenomena *cannot* be investigated physiologically, because physiologically nothing corresponds to them. (*RPP* §904, *Zettel* §609)

> I saw this man years ago: now I have seen him again, I recognize him, I remember his name. And why does there have to be a cause of this remembering in my nervous system? Why must something or other, whatever it might be, be stored-up there *in any form*? Why *must* a trace have been left? Why should there not be a psychological regularity to which *no* physiological regularity corresponds? (*RPP* §905, *Zettel* §610)

> The prejudice in favour of psycho-physical parallelism is . . . a fruit of the primitive conception of grammar. (*RPP* §906, *Zettel* §611)

Now, in fact, the bulk of the cognitive science the Second Philosopher relies on in her empirical treatment of logic doesn't obviously involve assumptions about the brain. Still, any speculation about evolutionary origins does assume that the causal history of the brain is relevant, and, in any case, of course the Second Philosopher regards physiological and neurological investigations as central to her broader study of human capabilities.[9] If Wittgenstein has a principled reason for ruling out such evidence, this would directly undercut the Second Philosopher's elaborations.

This theme slips into the *Investigations* itself in the discussion of reading, or more precisely, of a human being trained to read aloud.

> In the case of the live reading-machine, 'reading' meant: reacting to signs in such-and-such ways. So this concept was independent of that of a mental or other mechanism. . . . The change when the pupil began to read was a change in his *behaviour*. (*PI* §157)

The interlocutor retorts:

> But isn't that only because of our too slight acquaintance with what goes on in the brain and nervous system? If we had a more accurate knowledge of these things, we would see what connections were established by the training, and then when we

9. How the traditional philosopher's imaginary Martians might or might not accomplish similar tasks is of little second-philosophical interest.

> looked into his brain, we would be able to say: 'Now he has *read* this word, now the reading connection has been set up.' (*PI* §158)

The reply comes:

> And it presumably *must* be like that – for otherwise how could we be so sure that there was such a connection? That it is so is presumably a priori – or is it only probable? And how probable is it? Now, ask yourself: what do you *know* about these things? (*PI* §158)

Hacker, for one, takes this reply to be Wittgenstein's own, and its upshot to be that neural connections aren't part of the 'grammar' of reading – an idea that plays into his broader understanding of behavioral criteria versus hidden symptoms.[10] The analogous objection to the Second Philosopher's account of logic would presumably be that her work is focused on symptoms, not criteria, that she misses the true nature, the true 'grammar', of logical truth.

In light of the discussion of the purported 'specialness' of logic in the previous chapter, I think what we see here is another case of mistaking the voice of correctness for Wittgenstein himself. When such substantive conclusions are drawn from a philosophical distinction between 'criteria' and 'symptoms', we've clearly strayed into the realm of theory that Wittgenstein is so keen to avoid.

In contrast to Hacker, Robert Fogelin takes fierce exception to the reply in *PI* §158. He begins with 'what do you *know* about these things?':

10. See Baker and Hacker [2005], p. 335, 331. (Recall footnote 14 of chapter 6.) Again, it's worth noting that the ordinary notion of reading isn't what's at issue in *PI* §§157–158: the idea of a reading-machine is introduced and explicitly linked with behavior.

> Needless to say, we don't know very much about these things, and it is important to be skeptical of the advocates of artificial intelligence or computer simulation, who often confuse their research projects with results. (Fogelin [1987], p. 207)

In response to the question 'how probable is it?', he writes:

> But surely more than a prejudice lies behind the desire to find physiological explanations of psychological phenomena. In the first place . . . learning to read and developing the command of a concept through training are the kinds of phenomena for which explanation seems appropriate. This is not because they are odd or unusual; they just seem to be of the wrong *order* to be simply brute and inexplicable. In the same way, it would seem inappropriate to treat rain as one of the inexplicabilia of our world. (Imagine someone saying 'it just rains, that's all; explanation has to stop somewhere.') . . . Second, the assumption that these explanations may ultimately refer to the mechanism of the central nervous system only shows that we tend to return to a well that gives no signs of drying up. (Fogelin [1987], p. 207).

A first thought might be to cast Fogelin as the voice of temptation, opposite Hacker's voice of correctness, but notice that Fogelin hasn't claimed here to know anything a priori. In fact, what he offers is plain Second Philosophy: the successes of neuropsychology give us tentative reason to pursue explanations of this sort. The true voice of temptation, Wittgenstein's presentation suggests, would insist without empirical support that there *must* be something in the brain corresponding to 'reading', and perhaps even that there *must* be an (accessible?) explanation of the reader's behavior along these lines.

So I think that on a charitable interpretation of this passage from the *Investigations,* Wittgenstein isn't insisting on the irrelevance of physiology; despite appearances, he isn't directly engaging Fogelin or the Second Philosopher at all. Rather, he's concerned with a debate between the philosopher who claims to know without investigation that there *must* be an explanation of a certain kind, and the philosopher who denies this on grounds of the 'grammar' of psychological terms. Both make the mistake of thinking this sort of thing can be settled a priori. As for the less authoritative, more strident passages from *RPP* and *Zettel,* it seems reasonable to assume that if they'd been polished for appearance in more finished work, they would have found their way to the voice of correctness. Nothing here warrants taking Wittgenstein's avoidance of neuroscience as anything other than his general rejection of theorizing, the narrow scope of his therapeutic philosophy.[11]

A second proposal for motivating Wittgenstein's rejection of the Second Philosopher's empirical inquiries is based on the idea that human practices are too haphazard, too disordered, too unruly to support theorizing of any kind. This theme turns up in Stern's suggestion that

> Wittgenstein's unsystematic approach holds out the hope of doing justice to the indefinite and multi-colored filigree of everyday life. (Stern [2004], p. 167)

In his early book, Pears traces a similar line of interpretation:

11. Pears apparently agrees: 'Wittgenstein turns his face from neurology not because speakers of a language might have sawdust in their heads, but because, from the point of view of a philosopher with his restricted conception of the subject, it would not matter what they had in their heads' (Pears [1988], p. 513).

> [Wittgenstein] believed that the philosopher's presentation of linguistic examples should be like the work of an artist rather than the work of a scientist.[12] But, though it is evident to anyone who reads *Philosophical Investigations* that this is the way in which he saw his work, it is difficult to be sure of the precise points of analogy. (Pears [1969], p. 188)

> Complexity is one thing, and unanalyzable uniqueness is another thing,[13] and it may be that he thought that the meanings of things that people say are irreducibly particular. (Pears [1969], pp. 190–191)

> If someone is listening to a piece of music, and a theme makes a certain impression on him, he may be able to convey the impression to someone else, but not by the kind of analysis and generalization that would be appropriate in science. . . . [Wittgenstein] thought that [aesthetic appreciation and linguistic understanding] have a definite common factor: both involve the seeing of aspects, and to see an aspect is always to be aware of relations which reach out from the particular case in innumerable directions and give it its unique character. . . . He . . . thought these achievements of the human mind have a certain immunity from scientific analysis. (Pears [1969], pp. 192–193)

The idea might be, for example, that the various instances of following a rule are too idiosyncratic, too unique, to be captured by even the blandest generalization.

12. Cf. Pears [1969], p. 112: 'The task of collecting and arranging [individual facts about language] is more like the work of an artist than of a scientist.' Incidentally, Urmson ([1969], p. 25) reports that Austin took his method of investigating language to be 'empirical and scientific,' but that he admitted (quoting Austin now) that 'like most sciences, it is an art.'
13. Cf. Pears [1969], p. 33: 'No doubt, the truth in philosophy is very complex, but complexity is not unanalyzable uniqueness.'

Now it may be that beyond a few generalities about preferred shapes, color combinations, certain design elements, and the like, very little can be said in a theoretical way about human aesthetic response, about why I love this particular painting by Cezanne, but it's quite another thing to claim that nothing general can be said about why I think something either red or green that isn't red must be green. And, given the weight of what developmental psychologists have gleaned about conceptual development, psycholinguists about language learning, behavioral psychologists about group dynamics, and so on, it seems plain false to deny that generalization and theory can get a foothold in these areas. Of course, the Second Philosopher isn't out to corral every detail of our human practices, any more than a physicist, aiming to describe the flight of a cannonball, is out to include the individual bruises on each blade of grass in the field where it lands. But this by itself doesn't preclude the physicist's theories of motion or the cognitive scientist's investigation of various regularities in infants' reactions to experimental scenarios or the Second Philosopher's account of logic.

In fact I think there's a third version of a possible principled reason lurking behind this unconvincing one, as revealed in Stern's further discussion. He notes that one example of an explanatory theory of our practice would be a

> scientific account of its causal basis . . . placing it in a broader context of human behavior in naturalistic and causal terms. (Stern [2004], p. 168)

He continues:

> The point of such a theory of practice would be to provide a philosophical justification of our talk of meaning and understanding. (Stern [2004], p. 168)

'Justification' is the buzz word here. Above, both Pears and I have been at pains to acknowledge that the ordinary rule-follower stands under no obligation to provide anything beyond the ordinary justifications, which quickly run out. But again, that isn't the issue at this point. What we're asking now is: why shouldn't the Second Philosopher provide an explanatory account of what grounds the practice of rule-following, or more specifically, the practice of inferring – indeed, an account that simply fills in the various types of facts that Wittgenstein agrees do form its basis? If she can explain in this way why logical inference is reliable, she's happy to leave decisions about the appropriateness of the term 'justification' to the epistemologists; for example, if reliably formed belief is enough, presumably our rudimentary logical beliefs do count as justified. What's wrong with providing this sort of explanation/justification?[14]

I think the answer is that the kind of 'justification' being rejected isn't the kind of 'justification' the Second Philosopher offers. There's a hint of this in Stern's characterization:

> The anti-theoretical reading I have been outlining here is often known as 'quietism', for its denial that Wittgenstein has anything to say on the subject of grand philosophical theories about the relation between language and the world. (Stern [2004], p. 169)

Now the tip-off is the phrase 'grand philosophical theory'. Stern continues:

14. Here and in what follows I use 'explanation/justification' as shorthand for the Second Philosopher's explanation of the reliability of rudimentary logic, which may, for some epistemologists, also count as a justification.

> According to the quietist, Wittgenstein's invocation of forms of life is not the beginning of a positive theory of practice . . .

– as we've been taking it, from our second-philosophical perspective –

> but rather is meant to help his readers get over their addiction to theorizing about mind and world, language and reality. (Stern [2004], p. 169)

Presumably, on this reading, Wittgenstein isn't out to stop psychology or linguistics; what he hopes to cure is the impulse toward 'grand philosophical theories' of mind or language.

So what makes a theory 'grand' and 'philosophical'? Consider Pears's description of what Wittgenstein says the philosopher cannot do:

> He cannot describe a pre-existing situation and show that it forced us to adopt this particular rule. (Pears [1988], p. 255)

The Second Philosopher wouldn't say that the structure of the world 'forces' us to adopt rudimentary logic, but she does explain why we find it natural to do so and why this is largely a good thing, assuming we're out to track the truth. Pears goes on to explain why what he has in mind can't be done:

> That would require him to use language in order to get outside language, an impossible feat. (Pears [1988], p. 255)

This, I suggest, is what makes philosopher's theory, or attempted theory, 'grand': we're asked to explain how language or logic or scientific theory, viewed all at once, from outside, connects to the world, as it is in itself, in some raw, unconceptualized, noumenal state – and this obviously we cannot do, as there's no place to stand while doing it. But just as obviously, it isn't what the Second Philosopher aims to do: she begins her inquiry with ordinary perception and builds up from there by methodical observation, theory-formation and testing; her inquiry takes place within ordinary science, not in a 'grand philosophical' vacuum.[15] So once again, no objection to *her* efforts, to *her* way of gleaning explanation/justification from Wittgensteinian contingencies, has yet been found. Granted, it isn't the sort of explanation/justification that would persuade in all possible situations – it relies on features of our ordinary, contingent physical world – and thus not the sort of thing to satisfy the traditional philosopher, but that's as it should be.

Though discussion of these lines of thought hardly exhausts the secondary literature on this point, I hope it's enough to suggest that it's unlikely a persuasive case against the Second Philosopher's approach to the question of logical truth, against her explanation/justification of our inferential practices, is to be found in the late Wittgenstein's philosophy. We've seen four possible reasons for his anti-theoretical stand: the first restricts philosophy to an austere form of therapy, so that the Second Philosopher's account of logical truth must be relabeled as something else (though it's not clear what alternative description would be more appropriate); the second mistakes views of the voice of correctness for Wittgenstein's own; the third, based on the complexity of human behavior, draws an analogy with aesthetic judgment, an analogy that only

15. This is what's described in [2007] as the distinction between 'upper case' and 'lower case' theorizing (see 'capital letters' in the book's index). See also the discussion of Stroud's two skeptical arguments in §I.2, especially the second (pp. 29–33).

works if we ignore the successes of experimental psychology, cognitive science, and neuropsychology; and the fourth denounces a kind of justificatory undertaking quite different from what the Second Philosopher is actually up to.

There remains the possibility that Wittgenstein simply thinks that philosophical theorizing is a priori. Pears develops a version of this line of interpretation, starting from the late Wittgenstein's condemnation of the *Tractatus* for its

> .. curiously ambiguous status. On the one hand, it was established a priori and so it did not seem to need experimental verification. But on the other hand, it was supposed to have some sort of experiential status, if only on a very deep level of analysis, and that seemed to give it the explanatory power of a scientific theory. (Pears [1988], p. 206)

Pears suggests that

> [t]he effects of putting philosophical theorizing in quasi-scientific limbo are worth scrutinizing more closely. (Pears [1988], p. 206)

and he includes a broad range of theories under this rubric:

> The general mark of a theory of the type is the idea that the world imposes a fixed structure on our thought. (ibid.)

This sounds awfully strong, but it is true that the Second Philosopher takes our basic cognitive structures to be as they are because the world is the way it is. Pears continues:

> If we summed up Wittgenstein's case against philosophical theories at this point, it would be that they are postulates of reason rather than the experimental discoveries that they claim

> to be.... They are postulates that can never be verified, because their a priori status leaves no room for verification. (Pears [1988], p. 207)[16]

This should sound familiar: though more general in scope, it echoes the conclusion reached a few pages back in our discussion of the case of reading (especially *PI* §158). Wittgenstein has no objection to empirical investigation, but his focus is on how philosophy can go wrong, on the voices of temptation and correctness, and he criticizes them both for arguing a priori, whatever their pretense otherwise.

Now we've seen (in Chapter 2) that the Second Philosopher allows for some sense in which our simplest logical beliefs are a priori, but her account of why this is so is clearly empirical, open to confirmation, vulnerable to disconfirmation, in part or in its entirety. If the term 'philosophy' is reserved for a priori theorizing – whatever it might pretend to be – then again the Second Philosopher is practicing a successor discipline that addresses many traditional philosophical questions – like 'what is the ground of logical truth?' – using a new method. And again it's hard to see the point of this relabeling, but also pointless to quibble over a word.[17]

16. Pears goes on to trace two ways in which the case against philosophical theorizing in the *PI* 'goes beyond this point' (Pears [1988], p. 207), but these aren't directly relevant to the Second Philosopher. (One is Wittgenstein's argument against 'any theory that tries to put meaning on a static basis' (Pears [1988], p. 209). The other is his treatment of theorizing 'derived from ordinary, everyday experience' of privacy, culminating in the private language argument (Pears [1988], pp. 211–214).)

17. In his book on Hume, Stroud writes, 'It is the very idea of a completely comprehensive empirical investigation and explanation of why human beings are the way they are, and why they think, feel and behave as they do, that attracts [Hume's] philosophical attention' and 'only those who are both obsessed with compartmentalization and equipped with an adequate definition of philosophy will want to press ... the question of whether Hume is really doing philosophy or something else' (Stroud [1977], pp. 224, 8). Noble as Stroud's ideal here is, [2011b] casts doubt on the naturalistic credentials of Hume's execution.

To sum up, then, when it comes to justifying our inferential practices, Wittgenstein and the Second Philosopher agree that the ordinary rule-follower needs no more than the ordinary justifications, despite the fact that they soon give out; at the other extreme, they also agree that a 'grand philosophical' justification is neither promising nor required. Where they differ, if at all, is on the status of the Second Philosopher's intermediate form of explanation/justification: she claims that her investigations show what grounds our inferential practices (KF-structuring), how we come to find them natural (our basic cognitive machinery), and why adhering to them is a reliable way to find out about the world. Though Wittgenstein rejects this approach, we've been unable to locate any serious challenge to it among the various candidates for a principled Wittgensteinian reason to forbid appeal to science. If, in fact, it's just Wittgenstein's narrow conception of the nature of philosophy that prompts him to classify these second-philosophical considerations as something else, then on this reading, the two could agree on everything but the labels.

What this reading leaves out is Wittgenstein's personal antipathy to science, but this by itself carries no force. Nothing we've seen indicates that Wittgenstein's anti-theoretical stance is organically intertwined with the heart of the insights into rule-following and logical truth that he shares with the Second Philosopher. Here, then, is the thread to pull, the assumption to remove, in order to naturalize the late Wittgenstein's account of the logical must: the prohibition against science. Once that's gone, the road is clear for the elaboration proposed by the Second Philosopher.

Conclusion

I've argued that we can reach the vicinity of the second-philosophical view of logical truth by three very different routes: one by collapsing the empirical/transcendental distinction in Kant's account; a second by rejecting the assumption of the priority of sense from the early Wittgenstein's account in the *Tractatus*; and a third by removing the prohibition against scientific methods from the late Wittgenstein's account in the *Philosophical Investigations* and Part I of the *Remarks on the Foundations of Mathematics*.

In addition, we can now see our way out of the puzzle raised at the end of Chapter 4: given that the late Wittgenstein also rejects the priority of sense, why doesn't the late view immediately resemble the Second Philosopher's? The answer is that the late view also includes an additional feature, the ban on science, that blocks any second-philosophical development, even in the absence of the priority of sense. But it isn't as if this is an entirely new obstacle added to the late view even as the first obstacle was being removed; in fact, we now easily recognize that the rejection of science was present in the early work as well:[1]

> Philosophy is not one of the natural sciences. (4.111)

1. This was noted, but set aside, in chapter 4, to await the point we've now reached.

> Philosophy is not a body of doctrine but an activity. (4.112)
>
> Darwin's theory has no more to do with philosophy than any other hypothesis in natural science. (4.1122)

So, we now see, rejecting the priority of sense from the *Tractatus* in fact isn't enough by itself to bring the early view within reach of the Second Philosopher's position. What it does is bring the early view within reach of the late view, at which point the prohibition on science alone stands in our way.

My hope at the outset was that all this would shed light on Wittgenstein's views, so let me try to indicate what I think we've learned. On the *Tractatus,* because the focus was on isolating the key, non-naturalistic thread, we were led to examine the structure of the position from an unaccustomed angle, and what emerged was the central role the priority of sense plays in generating its more esoteric features: the hidden ontology of simples, the doctrine that every proposition represents a real possibility, and their downstream consequences. Without that presupposition, the picture theory remains – now based on the simple notion that the ordinary world has an objective logical structure. In this way we come to appreciate the pure logical realism of the view, independently of its abstruse elements.

Turning to the late Wittgenstein, the second-philosophical perspective highlights the dependence of our rule-following practices on very general features of the world, beginning with its KF-structure, as well as our interests and motivations, and our natural inclinations. And in light of our study of the *Tractatus,* we now easily recognize that what stands in the way of the troubled philosopher's appreciating the force of these ordinary facts is none other than his faith in the priority of sense. After this, rather surprisingly, we find Wittgenstein and the Second Philosopher arguing side by side on the contingency of logical truth, neither showing much sympathy for efforts to see logic as somehow special.

Finally, we could locate nothing of substance in Wittgenstein's rejection of science, of the kind of thing the Second Philosopher pursues to fill in their shared picture of what grounds our logical practices. This sets the third non-naturalistic thread in stark contrast to the first two: while the central motivations for Kant and the early Wittgenstein are lost in those respective naturalizing moves – the very priority phenomena the two of them set out to explain are seen to vanish in the second-philosophical context – nothing essential to the late Wittgenstein is lost when the prohibition against science is removed. In fact, the anti-scientific presumption seems more at home in his early view, where the entire project is so strongly a priori, than it does in the late view, where ordinary observations of ordinary practices in ordinary life take the spotlight. It's hard not to see it as a last lingering trace of Wittgenstein's earlier ways of thinking, no longer quite congenial in the new context.

One concluding note on that secondary aim, the promise of some insight into the Second Philosopher's views. Here I think the most remarkable discovery is how the Second Philosopher travels step by step through the rule-following considerations and the resulting, late-Wittgensteinian view of logic. Though her emphasis has been on the role of very general features of the world, she easily acknowledges the roles Wittgenstein assigns to our interests and motivations, and to our natural inclinations; she takes our logical practices to depend on these as well, just as our scientific practices do. So here is our final surprise: that a view as realistic and scientistic as the Second Philosopher's can actually accommodate the many subtle observations of the late Wittgenstein!

REFERENCES

Allison, Henry [2004] *Kant's Transcendental Idealism*, revised and enlarged edition (New Haven, CT: Yale University Press).

Austin, J. L. [1962] *Sense and Sensabilia*, G. J. Warnock, ed. (Oxford: Oxford University Press).

Baker, G. P. [2004] *Wittgenstein's Method*, K. Morris, ed. (Malden, MA: Blackwell).

Baker, G. P., and P. M. S. Hacker [2005] *Wittgenstein: Understanding and Meaning, Part II: Exegesis §§1–184* (Malden, MA: Blackwell). (First edition 1983; second edition, extensively revised by P. M. S. Hacker, 2005.)

Baker, G. P., and P. M. S. Hacher [2009] *Wittgenstein: Rules, Grammar and Necessity, Essays and Exegesis of §§185–242* (Malden, MA: Wiley-Blackwell). (First edition 1985; second edition, extensively revised by P. M. S. Hacker, 2009.)

Bloor, David [1996] 'Linguistic idealism revisited', in H. Sluga and D. Stern, eds., *Cambridge Companion to Wittgenstein* (Cambridge: Cambridge University Press), pp. 354–382.

Burge, Tyler [2000] 'Frege on a priority', reprinted in his [2005], pp. 356–387.

Burge, Tyler [2005] *Truth, Thought Reason* (Oxford: Oxford University Press).

Carnap, Rudolf [1950] 'Empiricism, semantics and ontology', reprinted in P. Benacerraf and H. Putnam, eds., *Philosophy of Mathematics*, second edition (Cambridge: Cambridge University Press, 1983), pp. 241–257.

Conant, James [1991] 'The search for logically alien thought', *Philosophical Topics* 20, pp. 115–180.

Cunning, David [2006] 'Descartes' Modal Metaphysics', *The Stanford Encyclopedia of Philosophy* (Summer 2011 Edition), Edward N. Zalta (ed.), URL = http://plato.stanford.edu/archives/sum2011/entries/descartes-modal/.

De Bary, Philip [2002] *Thomas Reid and Skepticism* (London: Routledge).

Descartes, René [1630] 'Letter to Mersenne, 27 May 1630', in his [1991], pp. 25–26.

Descartes, René [1644] 'Letter to Mesland, 2 May 1644', in his [1991], pp. 231–236.

Descartes, René [1991] *The Philosophical Writings of Descartes*, volume III, John Cottingham et al., eds. (Cambridge: Cambridge University Press).

Diamond, Cora [1986] 'Realism and the realistic spirit', reprinted in her *The Realistic Spirit* (Cambridge, MA: MIT Press, 1991), pp. 39–72.

Fogelin, Robert [1976] *Wittgenstein* (Boston: Routledge & Kegan Paul).

Fogelin, Robert [1987] *Wittgenstein*, second edition (London: Routledge).

Fogelin, Robert [2009] *Taking Wittgenstein at his Word* (Princeton, NJ: Princeton University Press).

Frankfurt, Harry [1977] 'Descartes on the creation of the eternal truths', *Philosophical Review* 86, pp. 36–57.

Frege, Gottlob [1879] *Begriffsschrift*, S. Bauer-Mengelberg, trans., reprinted in *From Frege to Gödel*, J. van Heijenoort, ed. (Cambridge, MA: Harvard University Press, 1967), pp. 5–82.

Frege, Gottlob [1880/1881] 'Boole's logical calculus and the concept-script', reprinted in his *Posthumous Writings*, H. Hermes, F. Kambartel, and F. Kaulbach, eds., P. Long and R. White, trans. (Chicago: University of Chicago Press, 1979), pp. 9–46.

Frege, Gottlob [1884] *Foundations of Arithmetic*, second revised edition, J. L. Austin, trans. (Oxford: Basil Blackwell, 1980).

Frege, Gottlob [1892] 'On Sinn and Bedeutung', reprinted in his [1997], pp. 151–171.

Frege, Gottlob [1893] *Grundgesetze dur Arithmetic*, volume 1, excerpted in his [1997], pp. 194–223.

Frege, Gottlob [1897] 'Logic', reprinted in his [1997], pp. 227–250.

Frege, Gottlob [1918/1919] 'Thought', reprinted in his [1997], pp. 325–345.

Frege, Gottlob [1997] *The Frege Reader*, M. Beaney, ed. (Oxford: Blackwell).

Gödel, Kurt [1932] 'On the intuitionistic propositional calculus', reprinted in his *Collected Works*, volume I, Solomon Feferman et al., eds. (New York: Oxford University Press, 1986), pp. 222–225.

Goldfarb, Warren[1985] 'Kripke on Wittgenstein on rules', reprinted in Miller and Wright [2002], pp. 92–107.

Hacker, P. M. S. [1986] *Insight and Illusion*, second edition (Bristol, UK: Thoemmes Press, 1997).

Hatfield, Gary [2003] 'Representation and constraints: the inverse problem and the structure of visual space', reprinted in his *Perception and Cognition* (Oxford: Oxford University Press, 2009), pp. 152–177.

Jackson, Frank [1998] *From Metaphysics to Ethics* (Oxford: Oxford University Press).

Kant, Immanuel [1772] 'Letter to Marcus Herz' in *Kant: Philosophical Correspondence 1759–99*, A. Zweig, trans. and ed. (Chicago: University of Chicago Press, 1967), pp. 70–76.

Kant, Immanuel [1781/1787] *Critique of Pure Reason*, P. Guyer and A. Wood, trans. and eds. (Cambridge: Cambridge University Press, 1997).

Kant, Immanuel [1800] *The Jäsche Logic*, in his *Lectures on Logic*, J. M. Young, trans. and ed. (Cambridge: Cambridge University Press, 1992), pp. 519–640.

Kripke, Saul [1965] 'Semantical analysis of intuitionistic logic I', in J. Crossley and M. Dummett, eds., *Formal Systems and Recursive Functions* (Amsterdam: North Holland), pp. 92–130.

Kripke, Saul [1982] *Wittgenstein on Rules and Private Language* (Cambridge, MA: Harvard University Press).

Kusch, Martin [2006] *A Sceptical Guide to Meaning and Rules: Defending Kripike's Wittgenstein* (Montreal: McGill-Queen's University Press).

Lear, Jonathan [1984] 'The disappearing "we"', *Proceedings of the Aristotelian Society*, supplementary volume 58, pp. 219–242.

Longuenesse, Béatrice [1993] *Kant and the Capacity to Judge*, C. T. Wolfe, trans. (Princeton, NJ: Princeton University Press, 1998).

MacFarlane, John[2002] 'Frege, Kant and the logic in logicism', *Philosophical Review* 111, pp. 25–65.

Maddy, Penelope[2007] *Second Philosophy* (Oxford: Oxford University Press).

Maddy, Penelope [2011a] 'Naturalism, transcendentalism and therapy', in J. Smith and P. Sullivan, *Transcendental Philosophy and Naturalism* (Oxford: Oxford University Press), pp. 120–156.

Maddy, Penelope [2011b] 'Naturalism and common sense', *Analytic Philosophy* 52, pp. 2–34.

Maddy, Penelope [2012] 'The philosophy of logic', *Bulletin of Symbolic Logic* 18, pp. 481–504.

Maddy, Penelope [2014] 'A second philosophy of arithmetic', to appear in the *Review of Symbolic Logic*.

Maddy, Penelope [201?] 'A second philosophy of logic', to appear in P. Rush, ed., *The Metaphysics of Logic* (Cambridge: Cambridge University Press).

McGinn, Marie[2006] *Elucidating the Tractatus* (Oxford: Oxford University Press).

Miller, Alexander, and Wright, Crispin, eds. [2002] *Rule-following and Meaning* (Montreal: McGill-Queen's University Press).

Monk, Ray [1990] *Ludwig Wittgenstein: the Duty of Genius* (New York: Penguin).

Morris, Michael [2008] *Wittgenstein and the Tractatus Logico-Philosophicus* (London: Routledge).

Papineau, David [2007] 'Naturalism', *The Stanford Encyclopedia of Philosophy (Spring 2009 Edition)*, Edward N. Zalta (ed.), URL = http://plato.stanford.edu/archives/spr2009/entries/naturalism/.

Pears, David [1969] *Ludwig Wittgenstein* (New York: Viking).

Pears, David [1981] 'Logical independence of elementary propositions', in I. Block, ed., *Perspectives on the Philosophy of Wittgenstein* (Oxford: Basil Blackwell), pp. 74–84.

Pears, David [1987] *The False Prison*, volume 1 (Oxford: Oxford University Press).

Pears, David [1988] *The False Prison*, volume 2 (Oxford: Oxford University Press).

Pears, David [2006] *Paradox and Platitude in Wittgenstein's Philosophy* (Oxford: Oxford University Press).

Prior, A. N. [1960] 'The runabout inference ticket', *Analysis* 21, pp. 38–39.

Putnam, Hilary [1968] 'Is logic empirical?', reprinted as 'The logic of quantum mechanics' in his *Mathematics, Matter and Method, Philosophical Papers*, volume 1, second edition (Cambridge: Cambridge University Press, 1979), pp. 174–197.

Putnam, Hilary [1983] 'Vagueness and alternative logic', reprinted in his *Realism and Reason, Philosophical Papers*, volume 3 (Cambridge: Cambridge University Press, 1983), pp. 297–314.

Quine, W. V. O. [1951] 'Two dogmas of empiricism', reprinted in his *From a Logical Point of View*, second edition (Cambridge, MA: Harvard University Press, 1980), pp. 20–46.

Reid, Thomas [1764] *An Inquiry into the Human Mind on the Principles of Common Sense*, D. R. Brookes, ed. (University Park: Pennsylvania State University Press, 1997).

Reid, Thomas [1785] *Essays on the Intellectual Powers of Man*, D. R. Brookes, ed. (University Park: Pennsylvania State University Press, 2002).

Rhees, Rush, ed.[1984] *Recollections of Wittgenstein* (Oxford: Oxford University Press).

Russell, Bertrand [1903] *Principles of Mathematics* (Cambridge: Cambridge University Press).

Russell, Bertrand [1910] 'On the nature of truth and falsehood', in his *Philosophical Essays* (London: Longmans, Green and Co.), pp. 170–185.

Russell, Bertrand [1912] *The Problems of Philosophy* (Oxford: Oxford University Press, 1959).

Russell, Bertrand [1913] *Theory of Knowledge* (London: Routledge, 1992).

Soames, Scott [2003] *Philosophical Analysis in the Twentieth Century*, volume 2, *The Age of Meaning* (Princeton, NJ: Princeton University Press).

Stalnaker, Robert [2001] 'Metaphysics without conceptual analysis', *Philosophy and Phenomenological Research* 62, pp. 631–636.

Stenius, Erik [1960] *Wittgenstein's Tractatus* (Oxford: Blackwell).

Stern, David [1994] 'Review essay: recent work on Wittgenstein, 1980–1990)', *Synthese* 98, pp. 415–458.

Stern, David [1995] *Wittgenstein on Mind and Language* (New York: Oxford University Press).

Stern, David [2003] 'The methods of the *Tractatus*', in P. Parrini et al, eds., *Logical Empiricism* (Pittsburgh, PA: Pittsburgh University Press), pp. 125–156.

Stern, David [2004] *Wittgenstein's Philosophical Investigations* (Cambridge: Cambridge University Press).

Stroud, Barry [1965] 'Wittgenstein and logical necessity', reprinted in his [2000], pp. 1–16.

Stroud, Barry [1977] *Hume* (London: Routledge and Kegan Paul).

Stroud, Barry [1983] 'Wittgenstein's "treatment" of the quest for "a language which describes my inner experiences and which only I myself can understand"', reprinted in his [2000], pp. 67–79.

Stroud, Barry [1984] 'The allure of idealism', *Proceedings of the Aristotelian Society*, supplementary volume 58, pp. 243–258, reprinted in his [2000b], pp. 83–98.

Stroud, Barry [2000] *Meaning, Understanding, and Practice* (Oxford: Oxford University Press).

Stroud, Barry [2000a] 'Private objects, physical objects, and ostension', in his [2000], pp. 213–232.

Stroud, Barry [2000b] *Understanding Human Knowledge* (Oxford: Oxford University Press).

Urmson, J. O. [1969] 'Austin's philosophy', in K.T. Fann, ed., *Symposium on J. L. Austin* (London: Routledge and Kegan Paul), pp. 22–32.

White, Roger [2006] *Wittgenstein's Tractatus Logico-Philosophicus* (London: Continuum).

Williamson, Timothy [1996] 'Putnam on the sorites paradox', *Philosophical Papers* 25, pp. 47–56.

Wilson, Margaret [1978] *Descartes* (London: Routledge).

Wittgenstein, Ludwig [1914–1916] *Notebooks 1914–1916*, second edition, G. E. M. Anscombe, trans., G. H. von Wright and G. E. M. Anscombe, eds. (Chicago: University of Chicago Press, 1979).

Wittgenstein, Ludwig [1921] *Tractatus Logico-Philosophicus*, C. K. Ogden, trans. (London: Routledge & Kegan Paul, 1922), and D. F. Pears and B. F. McGuinness, trans. (London: Routledge & Kegan Paul, 1961). (Translations cited in the text come from Pears and McGuinness unless otherwise noted.)

Wittgenstein, Ludwig [1933] *The Big Typescript*, C. Luckhardt and M. Aue, eds. (Malden, MA: Blackwell, 2005).

Wittgenstein, Ludwig [1932–1934] *Philosophical Grammar*, A. Kenny, trans., R. Rhees, ed. (Berkeley: University of California Press, 1974).

Wittgenstein, Ludwig [1933–1944] *Remarks on the Foundations of Mathematics*, revised edition, G. E. M. Anscombe, trans., G. H. con Wright, R. Rhees, and G. E. M. Anscombe, eds. (Cambridge, MA: MIT Press, 1978).

Wittgenstein, Ludwig [1945–1948] *Zettel*, G. E. M. Anscombe, trans., and G. E. M Anscombe and G. H. von Wright, eds. (Berkeley: University of California Press, 1970).

Wittgenstein, Ludwig [1947] *Remarks on the Philosophy of Psychology*, volume 1, G. E. M. Anscombe, trans., G. E. M. Anscombe and G. H. von Wright, eds. (Chicago, University of Chicago Press, 1980).

Wittgenstein, Ludwig [1949–1951] *On Certainty*, D. Paul and G. E. M. Anscombe, trans., G. E. M. Anscombe and G. H. von Wright, eds. (Oxford: Blackwell, 1969).

Wittgenstein, Ludwig [1953] *Philosophical Investigations*, revised fourth edition, G. E. M. Anscombe, P. M. S. Hacker, and Joachim Schulte, trans., P. M. S. Hacker and Joachim Schulte, eds. (Madlen, MA: Blackwell, 2009). This volume includes *Philosophy of Psychology, A Fragment*, formerly known as '*PI, Part* II'.

Wittgenstein, Ludwig [1980] *Culture and Value*, P. Winch, trans., G. H. von Wright and H. Nyman, eds. (Chicago: University of Chicago Press).

INDEX

Note: Locators followed by the letter 'n' refer to notes.